DOTTY DIMPLE STORIES.

DOTTY DIMPLE

AT HER GRANDMOTHER'S.

By SOPHIE MAY,

AUTHOR OF "LITTLE PRUDY STORIES."

Illustrated.

BOSTON:

LEE AND SHEPARD.

1868.

ELECTROTYPED AT THE
BOSTON STEREOTYPE FOUNDRY,
NO. 19 SPRING LANE.

Printing Statement:

Due to the very old age and scarcity of this book,
many of the pages may be hard to read due to the
blurring of the original text, possible missing pages,
missing text, dark backgrounds and other issues
beyond our control.

Because this is such an important and rare work, we
believe it is best to reproduce this book regardless of
its original condition.

Thank you for your understanding.

CONTENTS.

DOTTY DIMPLE AT HER GRAND-MOTHER'S.

CHAPTER I.

DOTTY'S PIN-MONEY.

EVERYTHING was very fresh and beautiful one morning in May, as if God had just made the world. The new grass had begun to grow, and the fields were dotted over with short, golden-topped dandelions.

The three Parlin children had come to their grandmother's much earlier in the season than usual; and now on this bright Sabbath morning they were going to church.

Dotty Dimple, otherwise Alice, thought

the fields looked like her aunt Maria's green
velvet toilet-cushion stuck full of pins.   The
spiders had spread their gauzy webs over the
grass, and the dew upon them sparkled in
the sunshine like jewels. "Such nice table-
cloths as they would have made for the
fairies," thought Dotty, "if there only were
any fairies."

"The world is ever so much handsomer
than it was a week ago," said Prudy, pointing towards the far-off hills.   "I'd like to be
on that mountain, and just put my hand out
and touch the sky."

"That largest pick," said Dotty, "is Mount
Blue.   It's covered with blueberries, and
that's why it's so blue."

"Who told you that?" asked Susy, smiling. "It isn't time yet for blueberries; and
if it was, we couldn't see them forty miles
off without a telescope."

"Jennie Vance told me," said Dotty ; "and she ought to know, for her father is the judge."

By this time the children had reached the church, and were waiting on the steps for the rest of the family. It was pleasant to watch the people coming from up and down the street, looking so neat and peaceful. But when Jennie Vance drew near with her new summer silk and the elegant feather in her hat, Dotty's heart gave a quick double beat, half admiration, half envy. Jennie's black eyes were shining with vanity, and her nicely gaitered feet tripped daintily up the steps.

"How d'ye do?" said she, carelessly, to Dotty, and swept by her like a little ship under full sail.

"Jennie Vance needn't talk so about her new mother," whispered Prudy, "for she gives her fifty-two new dresses, one for every Sunday."

Dotty's brow darkened. Just now it seemed to her one of the greatest trials in the whole world that the dress she wore had been made over from one of Prudy's. It was a fine white organdie with a little pink sprig, but there was a darn in the skirt. Then there was no feather in her hat, and no breastpin at her throat.

Poor Dotty! She did not hear much of the sermon, but sat very quiet, counting the nails in the pews and the pipes in the organ, and watching old Mr. Gordon, who had a red silk kerchief spread over his head to guard it against the draught from the window. She listened a little to the prayers, it is true, because she knew it was wrong to let her thoughts wander when Mr. Preston was speaking to God.

When the services were over, and she was
going to her Sabbath school class, she passed
Jennie Vance in the aisle.

"Where are you going, Jennie?" said she.

"Going home. My mamma says I needn't
stay to say my lessons and miss a warm dinner."

Jennie said this with such a toss of the
head that Dotty longed to reply in a cutting manner.

"It isn't polite to have warm dinners on
Sunday, Jennie Vance! But you said your
father had a *step-wife*, and perhaps she
doesn't know!"

"I didn't say my papa had a step-wife,
Dotty Dimple."

But this was all Jennie had time to retort,
for Dotty now entered the pew where her
class were to sit. Miss Preston was the
teacher, and it was her custom to have each

of her little pupils repeat a half dozen verses
or so, which she explained to them in a very
clear manner.   The children did not always
understand her, however; and you shall see
hereafter how Dotty's queer little brain grew
befogged.   The last clause of one of her
verses to-day was this : —

"The Lord loveth a cheerful giver."

"Suppose," said Miss Preston, "there were
two little girls living in a beautiful house,
with everything nice to eat and wear, and
there should come a poor man in rags, and
beg for charity.   One of the little girls is so
sorry for him that she runs to her mamma
and asks, as a favor, to be allowed to give
him some of her Christmas money.   The
other little girl shakes her head, and says,
'O, sister, what makes you do so?   But if
you do it *I* must.'   Then she pours out half
her money for the beggar, but scowls all the
while. — Which is the 'cheerful giver'?"

"The first little girl. O, of course, Miss
Preston." Then Dotty fell to thinking : —

"I don't have much to give away but just
pieces of oranges ; but I don't scowl when I
do it. I'm a great deal more 'cheerful' than
Jennie Vance ; for I never saw her give
away anything but a thimble after the pig
had chewed it. 'There, take it, Lu Piper,'
said she, 'for it pinches, and *I* don't want it.'
I shouldn't think *that* was very cheerful, I
am sure."

Thus Dotty treasured up the lesson for the
sake of her friend. It was really surprising
how anxious she was that Jennie should always do right.

Now it happened that before the week was
out a man came to Mr. Parlin's back door
begging. Dotty wondered if it might not
be the same man Miss Preston had men-
tioned, only he was in another suit of clothes.

She and Jennie were swinging, with Katie
between them, and Susy and Prudy were
playing croquet. They all ran to see what
the man wanted. He was not ragged, and
if it had not been for the green shade over
his eyes and the crooked walking-stick in his
hand, the children would not have thought
of his being a beggar. He was a very fleshy
man, and the walk seemed to have taken
away his breath.

"Little maidens," said he, in gentle tones,
"have you anything to give a poor tired
wayfarer?"

There was no answer, for the children did
not know what to say. But the man seemed
to know what to do; he seated himself on
the door-step, and wiped his face with a
cotton handkerchief. Little Katie, the girl
with flying hair, who was sometimes called
'Flyaway,' looked at him with surprise as he
puffed at every breath.

"When um breeves," said she to Dotty, "seems 's if um *uhissils*."

"Come here, little maiden," said the beggar, pointing to Dotty; "you are the handsomest of all, and you may take this document of mine. It will tell you that I am a man of great sorrows."

Dotty, very much flattered, took the paper from his hands. It was greasy and crumpled, looking as if it had been lying beside bread and butter in a dirty pocket. She gave it to Susy, for she could not read it herself. It was written by one of the "selectmen" of a far-away town, and asked all kind people to take pity on the bearer, who was described as "a poor woman with a family of children." Susy laughed, and pointed out the word "woman" to Prudy.

"Why do you smile, little ladies? Isn't it writ right? 'Twas writ by a lawyer."

"I will carry it in to my grandmother," said Susy; and she entered the house, followed by all the children.

"Who knows but he's a *griller?*" said Jennie.

"Lem *me* see paper," cried Katie, snatching at it, and holding it up to her left ear.

"O, dear!" sighed she, in a grieved tone; "it won't talk to me, Susy. I don't hear nuffin 'tall."

"She's a cunning baby, so she is," said Dotty. "She s'poses writing talks to people; she thinks that's the way they read it."

Grandmamma Parlin thought the man was probably an impostor. She went herself and talked with him; but, when she came back, instead of searching the closets for old garments, as Dotty had expected, she seated herself at her sewing, and did not offer to bestow a single copper on the beggar.

"Susy," said she, "he says he is hungry, and I cannot turn him away without food. You may spread some bread and butter, with ham between the slices, and carry out to him."

"What makes her so cruel?" whispered Dotty.

"O, grandma knows best," replied Prudy. "She never is cruel."

"What makes you put on so much butter?" said Jennie Vance; "I wouldn't give him a single thing but cold beans."

Dotty, whose Sunday school lesson was all the while ringing in her ears, looked at the judge's daughter severely.

"Would you pour cold beans into anybody's hands, Jenny Vance? Once my mamma gave some preserves to a beggar, —quince preserves, —she did."

Jennie only tossed her head.

"I'm going to give him some money," continued Dotty, defiantly; "just as cheerfully as ever I can."

"O, yes, because he called you the handsomest."

"No, Jennie Vance; because *I* am not stingy."

"Um isn't stinchy," echoed Katie.

"I've got some Christmas money here. I earned it by picking pins off the floor, six for a cent. It took a great while, Jennie, but *I* wouldn't be selfish, like *some* little girls!"

"Now, little sister," said Prudy, taking Dotty one side, "don't give your money to this man. You'll be sorry by and by."

But there was a stubborn look in Dotty's eyes, and she marched off to her money-box as fast as she could go. When she returned with the pieces of scrip, which amounted in

all to fifteen cents, the children were grouped
about the beggar, who sat upon the door-
step, the plate of sandwiches before him.

"Here's some money, sir, for your sick
children," cried Dotty, with an air of im-
portance.

"Blessings on your pretty face," replied
the man, eagerly.

Dotty cast a triumphant glance at Jennie.

"Ahem! This is better than nothing,"
added the beggar, in a different tone, after
he had counted the money. "And now
haven't any of the rest of you little maidens something to give a poor old wayfarer
that's been in the wars and stove himself up
for his country?"

There was no reply from any one of the
little girls, not even tender Prudy. And as
Dotty saw her precious scrip swallowed up
in that dreadfully dingy wallet, it suddenly

occurred to her that she had not done such a
very wise thing, after all.

"Why don't you eat your luncheon, sir?"
said Jennie Vance; for the man, after taking
up the slices of bread and looking at them,
had put them down again with an air of
disdain.

"I thought, by the looks of the house, that
Christians lived here," said he, shaking his
head slowly. "Haven't you a piece of apple
pie, or a cup custard, to give a poor man
that's been in prison for you in the south
country? Not so much as a cup of coffee or
a slice of beefsteak? No. I see how it is,"
he added, wiping his face and rising with an
effort; "you are selfish, good-for-nothing
creeters, the whole of you. Here I've been
wasting my time, and all I get for it is just
dog's victuals, and enough scrip to light
my pipe."

With this he began to walk off, puffing.
Dotty longed to run after him and call out,
"Please, sir, give me back my money."
But it was too late; and summoning all her
pride, she managed to crush down the tears.

"Tell the people in this house that I
shake off the dust of my feet against them,"
wheezed the stranger, indignantly. "The
dust of my feet — do you hear?"

"What a wicked, disagreeable old thing!"
murmured Jennie Vance.

"Dish-gwee-bly ole fing!" cried "Flyaway," nodding her head till her hair danced
like little tufts of corn-silk.

"I'm glad I didn't give him any of *my*
money," said Jennie, loftily.

"So am I," returned Susy.

Prudy said nothing.

"I didn't see him shake his feet," said
Dotty, changing the subject; "and the dust
wouldn't come off if he did shake 'em."

"Have you any more Christmas money left, Dotty?" said Jennie, twirling her gold ring on her finger.

"O, yes, ever so much at home.   And I shall soon have more," added Dotty, with a great effort to be cheerful; "for people are always dropping pins."

"I've got any quantity of scrip," pursued Jennie; "and I don't have to work for it, either."

"O, dear," thought Dotty, "what's the use to be good?   I 'sposed if I gave away my money *cheerfully*, they'd all feel ashamed of themselves; but they don't!   I wish I had it back in my box, I do!"

CHAPTER II.

PLAYING KING AND QUEEN.

"WHAT are you hunting for on your hands and knees, Alice?" said grandmamma, next day.

"O, nothing, only pins, grandma; but I can't find any. Isn't this a *hidden-mist* carpet?"

"No, dear; a *hit-and-miss* carpet is made of rags. But what do you want of pins?"

"She has given away what aunt Ria paid her for Christmas," said Prudy, speaking for her; "she gave it all to the beggar."

"Yes, she did; one, two, free, four, nineteen, tenteen," said Katie; "and the gemplum didn't love little goorls."

"Why, Alice! to that man who was here yesterday?"

Dotty was frowning at Prudy behind a chair. "Yes, 'm," she answered, in a stifled voice.

"Were you sorry for him?"

"No, ma'am."

"Did you hear me say I did not believe he was in need of charity?"

"Yes, 'm."

Grandma looked puzzled, till she remembered that Alice had always been fond of praise; and then she began to understand her motives.

"Did you suppose Jennie Vance and your sisters would think you were generous?" asked she, in a low voice.

Dotty looked at the carpet, but made no reply.

"Because, if that was your reason, Alice,

it was doing 'your alms before men, to be
seen of them.' God is not pleased when
you do so. I told you about that the other
day."

Still the little girl did not understand.
Her thoughts were like these : —

"Grandma thinks I'm ever so silly! Prudy thinks I'm silly! But isn't Jennie silly
too? And O, she takes cake, all secret, out
of her new mother's tin chest. I don't
know what will become of Jennie Vance!"

Mrs. Parlin was about to say more, when
Miss Flyaway, who had been all over the
house in two minutes, danced in, saying,
"the Charlie boy" had come!

It was little lisping Charlie Gray, saying,
"If you pleathe, 'm, may we have the Deacon
to go to mill? And then, if we may, can
you thpare uth a quart o' milk every thingle
night? Cauthe, if you can't, then you
muthn't."

Deacon was the old horse; and as Mr.
Parlin was quite willing he should go to
mill, Harry Gray came an hour afterwards
and led him away. With regard to the
other request, Mrs. Parlin had to think a
few minutes.

"Yes, Charlie," said she, at last; "you
may have the milk, because I would like to
oblige your mother; and you may tell her I
will send it every night by the children."

Now, Mrs. Gray was the doctor's wife.
She was a kind woman, and kept one closet
shelf full of canned fruit and jellies for sick
people; but for all that, the children did
not like her very well. Prudy thought it
might be because her nose turned up "like
the nose of a tea-kettle;" but Susy said it
was because she asked so many questions.
If the little Parlins met her on the street
when they went of an errand, she always

stopped them to inquire what they had been buying at the store, or took their parcels out of their hands and felt them with her fingers. She was interested in very little things, and knew how all the parlors in town were papered and carpeted, and what sort of cooking-stoves everybody used.

Dotty hung her head when her grandmother said she wished her to go every night to Mrs. Gray's with a quart of milk.

"Must I?" said she. "Why, grandma, she'll ask me if my mother keeps a girl, and how many tea-spoons we've got in the house; she will, honestly. Mayn't somebody go with me?"

"Ask me will I go?" said Katie, "for I love to shake my head!"

"And, grandma," added Dotty, "Mrs. Gray's eyes are so sharp, why, they're so sharp they almost prick! And it's no use for Katie to go with me, she's so little."

"O, I'm isn't *much* little," cried Katie. "I's growing big."

"I should think Prudy might go," said Dotty Dimple, with her finger in her mouth; "you don't make Prudy do a single thing!"

"Prudy goes for the ice every morning," replied Mrs. Parlin. "I wish you to do as I ask you, Alice, and make no more remarks about Mrs. Gray."

"Yes, 'm," said Dotty in a dreary tone; "mayn't Katie come too? she's better than nobody."

Katie ran for her hat, delighted to be thought better than nobody. The milk was put into a little covered tin pail. Dotty watched Ruth as she strained it, and saw that she poured in not only a quart, but a great deal more. "Why do you do so?" said Dotty. "That's too much."

"Your grandmother told me to," replied

Ruth, washing the milk-pail. "She said,
'Good measure, pressed down and running
over.' That's her way of doing things."

"But I don't believe grandma 'spected
you to press it down and run it *all* over.
Why, there's enough in this pail to make a
pound of butter. Come, Katie."

"Let me do some help," said the little one,
catching hold of the handle, and making the
pail much heavier. Dotty endured the weight
as long as she could; then, gently pushing
off the "little hindering" hand, she said, —

"And now, as we go along, we might as
well be playing, Flyaway."

"Fwhat?"

"Playing a play, dear. We'll make believe you're the queen with a gold crown on
your head."

Katie put her hand to her forehead.

"O, no, dear; you haven't anything on

your head now but the broadest-brimmedest
kind of a hat; we'll *call* it a crown.   And
I'm the king that's married to you."

"O, yes, mallied."

"And we're going — going — "

"Rouspin," suggested Flyaway.

"No: great people like us don't go rasp-
berrying.   Sit down here, Queenie, under
this acorn tree, and I'll tell you; we're going to the castle."

"O, yes, the cassil!"

"Where we keep our throne, dear, and
our gold dresses."

"Does we have any gold dollies to the
cassil?"

"O, yes, Queenie; all sizes."

"Does we have," continued Flyaway, wink-
ing slowly, "does we have — dip toast?"

"Why, Queenie, what should we want of
that?   Yes, we can have dip toast, I s'pose;

the girl can make it on the gold stove, with
a silver pie-knife. But we shall have nicer
things than ever you saw."

"Nicer than turnipers?"

"Pshaw! turnovers are nothing, Queenie;
we shall give them to the piggy. We shall
live on wedding cake and strawberries. Tea
and coffee, and such low things, we shall
give to ducks. O, what ducks they will
be! They will sing tunes such as canaries
don't know how. We'll give them our tea
and coffee, and we'll drink — what d'ye call
it? O, here's some."

Dotty took up the pail.

"You see how white it is; sugar frosting
in it. Drink a little, it's so nice."

"It tastes just like moolly cow's milk,"
said Flyaway, wiping her lips with her
finger.

"No," said Dotty, helping herself; "it's

nectar; that's what Susy says they drink; now I remember."

"Stop!" said a small voice in the ear of Dotty's spirit; "that is what I should call taking other people's things."

"Poh!" said Dotty, sipping again; "it's grandpa's cow. When Jennie Vance takes cake, it's wicked, because — because it is. This is only play, you know."

Dotty took another draught.

"Come, Queenie," said she, "let's be going to the castle."

Katie sprang up so suddenly that she fell forward on her nose, and said her foot was "dizzy." It had been taking a short nap as she sat on the stump; but she was soon able to walk, and shortly the royal pair arrived at the castle, which was, in plain language, a wooden house painted white.

"So you have come at last," said Mrs.

Gray, from the door-way.   "They don't milk very early at your house — do they?"

"No, ma'am, not so *very*."

"Have you seen anything of my little Charlie?"

"No, ma'am, not since a great while ago, — before supper."

"How is your grandfather?"

"Pretty well, thank you, ma'am."

"No, gampa isn't," said Katie, decidedly; "he's deaf."

"And what about your aunt Maria? Didn't I see her go off in the stage this morning?"

"Yes, 'm," replied Dotty, determined to give no more information than was necessary.

"She's gone off," struck in Katie; "gone to Dusty, my mamma has."

"Ah indeed! to Augusta?" repeated

3

Mrs. Gray, thoughtfully. "Any of your friends sick there?"

"No, ma'am," replied Dotty, scowling at her shoes.

"She's gone," continued Katie, gravely, "to buy me Free Little Kittens."

Mrs. Gray smiled. "I should think your mother could find kittens enough in this town, without going to Augusta. I thought I saw Horace on the top of the stage, but I wasn't sure."

Dotty made no reply.

"Hollis was," cried Katie, eagerly; "he goed to Dusty too. I fink they'll put Hollis in jail!"

"In jail!" exclaimed Mrs. Gray, throwing up her hands.

"He stealed, Hollis did," added Katie, solemnly.

"Hush, Katie, hush!" whispered Dotty

Dimple, seizing the child by the hand and
hurrying her away.   Mrs. Gray followed the
children to the door.

"What does she mean, Dotty! what can
she have heard?"

"She doesn't mean anything, ma'am,"
replied Dotty, beginning to run; "and she
hasn't heard anything, either."

Dotty's behavior was so odd, that Mrs.
Gray's curiosity was aroused.   For the moment she quite forgot her anxiety about her
little Charlie, who had been missing for some
time.

"What made you say Horace stole?" said
Dotty, as soon as they were out of hear-
ing.

"Hollis did," answered Katie, catching
her breath; "he stealed skosh seeds out of
gampa's razor cupboard."

"What did Horace want of squash seeds?"

"He eated em; I sawed him!"

"There, you're the funniest baby, Katie
Clifford! Now you've been and made Mrs.
Gray think your brother's carried to jail."

This was not quite true. Mrs. Gray had
no idea Horace had been taken to jail; but
she did fancy something had gone wrong at
Mr. Parlin's. She put on her bonnet and
ran across the road to Mrs. Gordon's, to ask
her what she supposed Horace Clifford had
been doing, which Dotty Dimple did not
wish to hear talked about, and which made
her run away when she was questioned.

"I can't imagine," said Mrs. Gordon, very
much surprised. "He is a frolicsome boy,
but I never thought there was anything
wicked about Horace."

Then by and by she remembered how
Miss Louise Parlin had lost a breastpin in
a very singular manner, and both the ladies
wondered if Horace could have taken it.

"One never can tell what mischief children may fall into," said Mrs. Gray, rubbing her left cheek-bone; "and that reminds me how anxious I am about my little Charlie; he ought to have been at home an hour ago."

While Mrs. Gray was saying this in Mrs. Gordon's parlor, there was a scene of some confusion in Mr. Parlin's door-yard.

"Who's this coming in at the gate?" cried Dotty.

It was Deacon, but Deacon was only a part of it; the rest was two meal-bags and a small boy. The meal-bags were full, and hung dangling down on either side of the horse, and to each was tied a leg of little Charlie Gray. It was droll for a tiny boy to wear such heavy clogs upon his feet, but droller still to see him resting his curly head upon the horse's mane.

"Ums the Charlie boy," said Katie; "um can't sit up no more."

"Ah, my boy, seems to me you take it very easy," said Abner, who was just coming in from the garden, giving some weeds a ride in the "one-wheeled coach," or wheelbarrow.

"Why don't you hold your head up, darling?" said Dotty.

"O, bring the camphor," screamed Susy; "he's fainted away! he's fainted away!"

"Not exactly," said Abner, untying the strings which held him to the bags. "Old Deacon has done very well this time; the boy is sound asleep."

As soon as Abner had wheeled away his weeds, he mounted the horse and trotted to Mrs. Gray's with the meal-bags, singing for Katie's ear, —

" Ride away, ride away; Charlie shall ride;
  He shall have bag of meal tied to one side;
  He shall have little bag tied to the other,
  And Charlie shall ride to see our grandmother."

The little boy stood rubbing his eyes.

"Why, Charlie, darling," said Prudy, "who tied you on?"

"The man'th boy over there. Hally didn't come cauthe he played ball; and then the mau'th boy tied me on."

Charlie made up a lip.

"Let's take him out to the swing," said Prudy. "That will wake him up, and then we'll make a lady's chair and carry him home."

"Don't want to thwing," lisped Charlie.

"What for you don't?" said wee Katie.

"Cauthe the ladieth will thee me."

"O, you's a little scat-crow!"

"Hush, Katie," said the older children; "do look at his hair; it curls almost as tight as dandelion stems."

"Thee the dimple in my chin!"

"Which chin?" said Prudy; "you've got three of them."

"And the wuffle wound my neck! Gueth what we've got over to my houthe? Duckth."

"O, ducks?" cried Dotty; "that's what I want to make me happy. There, Prudy, think of their velvet heads and beads of eyes, waddling about this yard."

"People sometimes take ducks' eggs and put them in a hen's nest," said Prudy, reflectively.

"O, there, now," whispered Dotty, "shouldn't you think Mrs. Gray might give me three or four eggs for carrying the milk every single night?"

"Why, yes, I should; and perhaps she will."

"I gueth my mamma wants me at home," said Charlie, yawning.

Prudy and Dotty went with him; and in her eagerness concerning the ducks' eggs, Dotty quite forgot the secret draughts of milk she and Katie had quaffed under the acorn-tree, calling it nectar. But this was not the last of it.

CHAPTER III.

THE WHITE TRUTH.

DOTTY continued to go to Mrs. Gray's every night with the milk. Sometimes Katie went with her, and then they always paused a while under the acorn-tree and played "King and Queen." Dotty said she wished they could ever remember to bring their nipperkins, for in that case the milk would taste a great deal more like nectar. The "nipperkins" were a pair of handled cups which the children supposed to be silver, and which they always used at table.

Dotty knew she was doing wrong every time she played "King and Queen." She

knew the milk was not hers, but Mrs.
Gray's; still she said to herself, "Ruthie
needn't give so much measure, all pressed
down and run over. If Queenie and I
should drink a great deal more, there would
always be a quart left. Yes, I know there
would."

Mrs. Gray never said anything about the
milk; she merely poured it out in a pan, and
gave back the pail to Dotty, asking her at
the same time as many questions as the child
would stay to hear.

One night Dotty begged Prudy to go with
her; she wished her to ask for the ducks'
eggs. When they reached the acorn tree
Dotty did not stop; she would never have
thought of playing "King and Queen" with
Prudy; she was afraid of her sister's honest
blue eyes.

I am not quite sure Mrs. Gray would have

given the eggs to Dotty, though Mrs. Parlin
promised her several times the amount of
hens' eggs in return. Mrs. Gray did not
think Dotty was "a very sociable child;"
and then so many people were asking for
eggs! But Mrs. Gray could not say "No"
to Prudy; she gave her thirteen eggs, with
a hearty kiss.

"Now whose will the ducklings be?" asked
Dotty on the way home.

"Yours and mine," replied Prudy; "half
and half. Six for each, and an odd one
over."

"Then," said Dotty, "we'll give that 'odd
one over' to Katie."

"But they may not all hatch, Dotty."

"O, dear! why not? Then we can't tell
how many we shall have. Perhaps there
will be two or three odd ones over; and
then what shall we do, Prudy?"

Prudy laughed at the idea of "two or three odd ones." The eggs were put in a barrel under the white hen; and now began a trial of patience. It seemed to all the children that time stood still while they waited. Would the four weeks never be gone?

One day Dotty stood with Katie by the back-door blowing bubbles. The blue sky, the white fences, the green trees, and even the people who passed in the street, made little pictures of themselves on the bubbles. It was very beautiful. Dotty blew with such force that her cheeks were puffed as round as rubber balls. Katie looked on in great delight.

"See," she cried, "see the trees a-yidin' on that bubbil!"

Dotty dropped the pipe and kissed her.

"Dear me," said she next minute, "there's Miss Polly coming!"

Katie looked along the path, and saw a
forlorn woman tightly wrapped in a brown
shawl, carrying a basket on her arm, and
looking sadly down at her own calf-skin
shoes, which squeaked dismally as she
walked.

"Is um the Polly?" whispered Katie; "is
um so tired?"

"No, she isn't tired," said Dotty; "but
she feels dreadfully all the whole time; I
don't know what it's about, though."

By this time the new-comer stood on the
threshold, sighing.

"How do you do, you pretty creeturs?"
said she, with a dreary smile.

"Yes, um," replied Katie; "is you the
Polly, and does you feel drefful?"

The sad woman kissed the little girls, —
for she was fond of children, — sighed more
heavily than ever, asked if their grandmothe-

was at home, and passed through the kitchen on her way to the parlor.

Mrs. Parlin sat knitting on the sofa, Mrs. Clifford was sewing, and Miss Louise crocheting. They all looked up and greeted the visitor politely, but it seemed as if a dark cloud had entered the room. Miss Polly seated herself in a rocking-chair, and began to take off her bonnet, sighing as she untied the strings, and sighing again as she took the three pins out of her shawl.

"I hope you are well this fine weather," said Mrs. Parlin, cheerily.

"As well as I ever expect to be," replied Miss Polly, in a resigned tone.

Then she opened the lids of her basket with a dismal creak, and took out her knitting, which was as gray as a November sky. Afterwards she slowly pinned a corn-cob to the right side of her belt, and began to knit.

At the end of every needle she drew a deep
breath, and felt the stocking carefully to
make sure there were no "nubs" in it. She
talked about the "severe drowth" and some
painful cases of sickness, after which she
took out her snuff-box, and then the three
ladies saw that she had something particular
to say.

"Where is your little boy, Maria?"

She always called Mrs. Clifford Maria, for
she had known her from a baby.

"Horace is at Augusta; I left him there
the other day."

"Yes," said Polly, settling her mournful
black cap, "so I heard! I was very, very
sorry," and she shook her head dolefully, as
if it had been a bell and she were tolling it
—"very, very sorry!"

Mrs. Clifford could not but wonder why.

"It is a dreadful thing to happen in a

family! I'm sure, Maria, I never heard that stealing was natural to either side of the house!"

"Stealing!" echoed Mrs. Clifford.

"What in this world can you mean, Polly Whiting?" said aunt Louise, laughing nervously; for she was a very lively young lady, and laughed a great deal. Miss Whiting thought this was no time for jokes. Her mouth twitched downward as if there were strings at the corners. Mrs. Clifford had turned very pale.

"Polly," said she, "do speak, and tell me what you have heard? It is all a mystery to me."

"You don't say so," said Miss Whiting, looking relieved. "Well, I didn't more than half believe it myself; but the story is going that your Horace stole his aunt Louise's breast-pin, and sold it to a pedler for a rusty gun."

4

Miss Louise laughed merrily this time.

"I did lose my pearl brooch," said she; "but Prudy found it yesterday in an old glass candlestick."

"What an absurd report!" said Mrs. Clifford, quite annoyed. "I hope the children are not to be suspected every time their *aunt Louise* misses anything!"

"They said you had decided to take Horace to the Reform School," added Miss Whiting, "but your friends begged you to leave him at Augusta in somebody's house, locked up, with bread and water to eat."

"Now tell me where you heard all this," said aunt Louise.

"Why, Mrs. Grant told me that Mrs. Small said that Mrs. Gordon told *her.* I hope you'll excuse me for speaking of it; but I thought you ought to know."

Miss Polly Whiting was a harmless wo-

man, who went from family to family doing
little "jobs" of work. She never said what
was not true, did no mischief, and in her
simple way was quite attached to the Parlins.

"I heard something more that made me
very angry," said she, following Miss Louise
into the pantry. "Mrs. Grant says Mrs.
Gray is very much surprised to find your
mother doesn't give good measure when she
sells milk!"

Aunt Louise was so indignant at this that
she went at once and told her mother.

"It is a little too much to be borne," said
she; "the neighbors may invent stories
about Horace, if they have nothing better
to do, but they shall not slander my
mother!"

The two little girls, who were the unconscious cause of all this mischief, were just
returning from Mrs. Gray's.

"O, grandma," said Dotty, coming in
with the empty pail; "she says she don't
want any more milk this summer, and I'm
ever so glad! Come, Prudy, let's go and
swing."

"Stop!" said Mrs. Parlin; "why does
Mrs. Gray say she wants no more milk?"

"'Cause," replied Dotty, "'cause our cow
is dry, or their cow is dry, or Mrs. Gordon
has some to sell. I don't know what she
told me, grandma; I've forgot!"

"Then, my dear, she did not say you
brought too little milk?"

Dotty winced. "No, grandma, she never."

"Ruth," said Mrs. Parlin, "you are sure
you have always measured the milk in that
largest quart, and thrown in a gill or two
more, as I directed?"

"O, yes, ma'am, I've never failed."

"Then I'm sure I cannot understand it,"

said Mrs. Parlin, her gentle face looking troubled.

"Unless the children may have spilled some," remarked Mrs. Clifford. "Dotty, have you ever allowed little Katie to carry the pail?"

"No, Dotty don't; her don't 'low me care nuffin — there now!" cried Katie, very glad to tell her sorrows.

"She's so little, you know, aunt 'Ria," murmured Dotty, with her hand on the door-latch.

There was a struggle going on in Dotty's mind. She wished very much to run away, and at the same time that "voice" which speaks in everybody's heart was saying, —

"Now, Dotty, be a good girl, a noble girl. Tell about drinking the milk under the acorn tree."

"But I needn't," thought Dotty, clicking

the door-latch! "it won't be a fib if I just
keep still."

"Yes, it will, Dotty Dimple!"

"What! When I squeeze my lips together and don't say a word?"

"'Twill be *acting* a fib, and you know it,
Alice Parlin! I'm ashamed of you! Take
your fingers out of your mouth, and speak
like a woman."

"I will, if you'll stop till I clear my
throat. — O, grandma," cried Dotty, "I
can't tell fibs the way Jennie Vance does!
'Twas we two did it, as true as you live!"

"Did what, child? Who!"

"The milk."

"I don't understand, dear."

Dotty twisted the corner of her apron,
and looked out of the window.

"Drank it — Katie and me — under the
acorn tree."

"Yes, she did," chimed in Katie; "and 'twasn't nuffin but moolly cow's milk, and her 'pilled it on my shoe!"

Grandmamma really looked relieved.

"So this accounts for it! But Dotty, how could you do such a thing?"

"I telled um not to," cried Katie, "but her kep' a-doin' an' a-doin'."

"Ruthie gives too much measure," replied Dotty, untwisting her apron—"'most two quarts; and when Katie and I ask for some in our nipperkins, Ruthie says, 'No,' she must make butter. I was just as thirsty, grandma, and I thought Mrs. Gray never would care; I did certainly."

"Yes, gamma, we fought Mis Gay would care; did cerdily!"

"My dear Dotty," said Mrs. Parlin, "you had not the shadow of a right to take what belonged to another. It was very wrong;

but I really believe you did not know how
wrong it was."

Dotty began to breathe more freely.

"But you see, child," interposed aunt
Louise, "you have done a deal of mischief;
and I must go at once to Mrs. Gray's and
explain matters."

Dotty was distressed at the thought of
Mrs. Gray, whose nose she could seem to
see "going up in the air."

"Don't feel so sorry, little sister," said
Prudy, as they walked off with their arms
about each other's waist; "you didn't do
just right, but I'm sure you've told the real
white truth."

"So I have," said Dotty, holding up her
head again; "and mother says that's worth
a great deal!"

CHAPTER IV.

DOTTY'S CAMEL.

MATTERS were soon set right with Mrs. Gray, who was sorry she had not spoken frankly to Mrs. Parlin in the first place, instead of going secretly to the neighbors and complaining that she did not receive her due allowance of milk. Perhaps it was a good lesson for the doctor's wife; for she ceased to gossip about the Parlins, and even took the pains to correct the wrong story with regard to the pearl breastpin.

After this Dotty and Katie carried the milk as usual; only they never stopped under the acorn tree any more to play "King

and Queen." Not that Dotty felt much
shame. She held herself in high esteem.
She knew she had done wrong, but thought
that by telling the truth so nobly she had
atoned for all.

"I am almost as good as the little girls in
the Sunday school books," said she; "now
there's Jennie Vance — I'm afraid she fibs."

Jennie called one day to ask Dotty and
Flyaway to go to school with her.

"Jennie," said Miss Dimple, gravely, as
they were walking with Katie between them,
"do they ever read the Bible to you?"

"Yes; why?"

"O, nothing; only you don't act as if you
knew anything about it."

"I guess my mother is one of the first
ladies in this town, Miss Dimple, and she's
told me the story of Joseph's coat till I
know it by heart."

"Well," said Dotty, looking very solemn; "it hasn't done you any good, Jennie Vance. Now, I learn verses every Sunday, and one is this: 'Lie not one to another.' What think of that?"

Jennie's black eyes snapped. "I heard that before ever you did."

"Lie not one to another," repeated Dotty, slowly. "Now, I'm *one*, Jennie, and you're *another;* and isn't it wicked when we tell the leastest speck of a fib?"

"Of course 'tis," was the prompt reply; "but I don't tell 'em."

"O, Jennie, who told your step-mother that Charlie Gray was tied up in a meal-bag? I'm afraid," said Dotty, laying her hand solemnly on little Katie's head as if it had been a pulpit-cushion, and she a minister preaching, — "I'm afraid, Jennie, *you* lie one to another."

"One to anudder," echoed Katie, breaking away and running after a toad. Jennie knitted her brows. "It doesn't look very well for such a small child as you are to preach to me, Dot Parlin!"

"But *I* always tell the white truth myself, Jennie, because God hears me. Do *you* think much about God?"

"No, I don't know as I do; nobody does, He's so far off," said Jennie, stooping to pluck an innocent flower.

"Why, Jennie, He isn't far off at all! He's everywhere, and here too. He holds this world, and all the people, right in His arms; right in His arms, just as if 'twas nothing but a baby."

Dotty's tones were low and earnest.

"Who told you so?" said Jennie.

"My mamma; and she says we couldn't move nor breathe without Him not a minute."

"There, I did then!" cried Jennie, taking a long breath; "I breathed way down ever so far, and I did it myself."

"O, but God let you."

Dotty felt very good and wise, and as she had finished giving her benighted friend a lesson, she thought she would speak now of every-day matters.

"Look at those little puddles in the road," said she; "don't they make you think of pudding-sauce — molasses and cream, I mean — for hasty-pudding?"

"No," said Jennie, tossing her head, "I never saw any pudding-sauce that looked a speck like that dirty stuff! Besides, we don't use molasses at our house; rich folks never do; nobody but poor folks."

"O, what a story!" said Dotty, coloring. "I guess you have molasses gingerbread, if your father *is* the judge!"

Dotty was very much wounded. This was not the first time her little friend had referred to her own superior wealth. "Dear, dear! Wasn't it bad enough to have to wear Prudy's old clothes, when Jennie had new ones and no big sister? She's always telling hints about people's being poor! Why, my papa isn't *much* poor, only he don't buy me gold rings and silk dresses, and my mamma wouldn't let me wear 'em if he did; so there!"

By the time they reached the school-house, Dotty was almost too angry to speak. They took their seats with Katie between them (when she was not under their feet or in their laps), and looked over in the Testament. The large scholars "up in the back seats," and in fact all but the very small ones, were in the habit of reading aloud two verses each. This morning it was the nineteenth chapter of Matthew, and Dotty paid little heed till her ear was caught by these words, read quite slowly and clearly by Abby Grant : —

"Then said Jesus unto his disciples, Verily I say unto you, that a rich man shall hardly enter the kingdom of heaven.

"And again I say unto you, It is easier for a camel to go through the eye of a needle than for a rich man to enter into the kingdom of God."

Dolly's heart gave a great bound. That meant Judge Vance just as sure as the world. Wasn't he rich, and didn't Jennie boast of it as if it was a great thing? She touched her friend's arm, and pointed with her small forefinger to the passage ; but Jennie did not understand.

"It isn't my turn," whispered she ; "what are you nudging me for?"

"Don't you see your papa isn't going to heaven?" said Dotty. "God won't let him in, because he's rich."

"I don't believe it," said Jennie, quite un-moved.

"O, but God won't, for the Bible says so. He can't get in any more than a camel can get into a needle; and you know a camel can't."

"But the needle can go into a camel," said Jennie, thoughtfully; "perhaps that's what it means."

"O, no," whispered Dotty. "I know bet-ter'n that. I'm very sorry your papa is rich."

"But he isn't so very rich," said Jennie, looking sober.

"You always said he was," said Dotty, with a little triumph.

"Well, he isn't rich enough for *that!*

He's only rich a little mite,—just a little teenty tonty mite," added Jennie, as she looked at Dotty's earnest face, and saw the rare tear gathering on her eyelashes.

"But *my* father isn't rich the least bit of a speck," said Dotty, with a sudden joy. "Nobody ever said he was. Not so rich, at any rate, Jenny, but you could put it through a needle. You could put it through a needle just as easy."

Jennie felt very humble—a strange thing for her. This was a new way of looking at things.

"Of course *he'll* go to heaven, you know," said Dotty; "there's no trouble about that."

"I s'pose he will," sighed Jennie, looking at her beautiful gold ring with less pleasure than usual. She had been in the habit of twirling it about her finger, and telling the little girls it was made of real "carrot gold."

But just at this moment she didn't care so
much about it; and it even seemed to her
that Dotty's little hand looked very nice and
white without any rings. Perhaps people
had not admired the glitter of her forefinger
so very much, after all. How did she know
but they had said, "Look at Judge Vance's
little daughter. Isn't she ashamed to wear
that ring when it's a sign her father is rich,
and can't go to heaven?" The child began to wish there would come holes in her
father's pockets and let out the money; for
she supposed he kept it all in his pockets,
of course.

"I shall tell my mother about it," mused
she; "and I don't believe but she'll laugh
and say, 'That Dotty Dimple is a very queer
child.'"

But just at this time little Katie began to
peep into Jennie's pockets for "candy-seeds"

(that is, sugared spices), and to behave in
many ways so badly that Miss Prince said
she must be taken home. So the girls led
her out between them; and that was the last
Jennie thought of the camel. But Dotty
remembered it all the way home.

CHAPTER V.

A SAD FRIGHT.

But the next afternoon, as the two little girls were walking home together, Dotty said to Jennie, with a very wise face, —

"Grandma has told me what the Bible means. Now I understand every single thing."

Jennie did not seem as much delighted as had been expected.

"She says God can get that camel through a needle."

"O, I remember," said Jennie; "you mean that Bible camel."

"There isn't anything he can't do," continued Dotty; "the richest men, richer than your father, can get to heaven if God's a mind to take 'em."

"Not bad people," said Jennie, shaking her head.

"I don't know about that; she didn't say," said Dotty, looking puzzled. "O, no, I s'pose not. God wouldn't be a mind to. For don't you see, Jennie Vance, it's just *like* a camel. There can't anybody go through themselves unless God *pulls* 'em through."

I don't know what grandmamma Parlin would have thought if she had heard her words chopped up in this way; but it made very little difference to Jennie, who paid no attention at all.

"Your father'll get there," added Dotty; "so I thought I'd tell you."

"Your shoestring's untied," said Jennie, coolly.

"And I don't care now if you are the richest," said Dotty, stooping to tie the string; "for God loves me just as well when I wear Prudy's old things; and so do all the good people in this town, and the minister too; grandma said so. I don't care how much you talk about our old Deacon, or our eating molasses. That isn't anything! Grandma says it's harder for rich children to be good, and I told her I was real glad I was half-poor."

"You're stepping right in the mud," cried Jennie.

"And then grandma said that it didn't make any difference any way about that, if I only loved God; but if I didn't love God, it did."

"There," said Jennie, "I haven't heard half you've said; and I guess you've forgotten all about going strawberrying."

"I almost know grandma won't be willing," replied Dotty; "we've got company, too; see those ladies in the window."

"All the better," replied Jennie, cheerily. "You go in and behave as beautifully as ever you can, and your grandma 'll be so busy talking, she'll say yes before she thinks. That's the way my mamma does. Say 'Crossman's orchard,' remember, but don't tell which one."

So Jennie staid outside while Dotty entered the parlor softly, and stood by her grandmother's chair, waiting the proper time to speak.

"Strawberrying, did you say?" asked Mrs. Parlin, presently.

"Yes, grandma; the berries are just as thick."

"O, just as fick!" repeated Katie, clapping her hands.

"In the Crossman orchard," added Dotty.

"Prosser Horcher," put in Katie, choking a little at the large words. "May her, gamma?"

Now, Dotty knew, as her grandmother did not, that there were two orchards; and the one she meant was a mile and a half away.

"Yes, you may go, Alice; it is only a few steps; but put on an old dress, and don't stay late; you know you are hardly well since your sore throat."

Dotty had not actually told a wrong story, but for almost the first time she had deceived, and she knew the sin was the same. While she was exchanging her pretty pink frock for one of dark calico, her conscience pricked so painfully that she almost wished to stay at home.

"Just as soon as we get out of the village," said Jennie, "I'm going barefoot; mother said I might."

"How splendid your mother is!" sighed
Dotty. "Grandma's so particular! But
any way I'm going without my stockings; I
declare I will. My throat's so far away
from my feet, what hurt will it do?"

"Children, obey your parents," said the
troublesome voice.

"Grandma isn't my parent," thought Dotty, tugging away at her boot-lacings. They
went out through the kitchen, to get Dotty's
red and white picnic basket; but they crept
like a pair of thieves, lest Ruthie, who was
mixing waffles, should hear them, and take
notice of Dotty's bare ankles.

Once out of the village, it did not take
long for Miss Dimple to slip off her boots
and tuck them in her pocket.

"O, how nice and cool!" murmured she,
poking her little pink toes into the burning
sand; till presently, a thorn, which ap-

peared to be waiting for that very purpose, thrust its way deep into her foot. She sat down in the middle of the road and screamed. Jennie tried her best to draw out the thorn, but only succeeded in breaking it off. Then, with a clumsy pin, she made a voyage of discovery round and round in the soft flesh of Dotty's foot, never hitting the thorn, or coming anywhere near it.

"O, dear!" said Jennie, petulantly; "we've wasted half an hour! What's the use for you to be always getting into trouble? A great many berries we shall have at this rate! and I was going to ask my mamma to let me have a party."

"There!" said Dotty, bravely, "I'm going right along now, and no more fuss about it."

It was hard work; Dotty limped badly; and all the while the cruel thorn was triumphantly working its way farther in. The Crossman orchard was not very far away now; but when they had reached it, and had crept under the fence, why, where were the strawberries? What the boys had not gathered they had trampled down; and the truth was, there had been very few in the first place. There was nothing to do but pluck here and there a stray berry, and make the most of it.

"This is what I call a shame," sighed Jennie; "and look at the sky; it's growing as black as a pickpocket."

"Why, yes," moaned Dotty; "how fast that sun has gone down!"

But this was a mistake. It was only six o'clock. The sun, understanding his business perfectly, had not hurried one jot. The clouds were merely spreading a dark background for some magnificent fireworks; in other words, a thunder-shower was coming up.

"Let's go right straight home," said Jennie; and Dotty was glad to hear the words, for in her own brave little heart she had determined not to be the first to surrender.

"Let's go across the fields," she replied; "it's the nearest way home."

By this time heavy drops were pattering down on the long grass, and making a hollow sound on the little girls' hats.

"Why, it's raining," remarked Dotty.

"You don't say so," sniffed Jennie, whose temper was quite upset; "perhaps you think you're telling some news."

Then came the frightful boom of thunder.

"What's that?" whispered Dotty, with white lips. "I'm afraid, Jennie; I certainly am."

"For shame, Dotty Dimple! I thought

you were the girl that knew all abo God
and the Bible. I shouldn't think you'd be
afraid of thunder!"

"O, but I am!" was the meek reply.
"I'm as afraid as I can live."

"There, hush up, Dotty! When you've
been and got us into a fix, you'd better keep
still."

"I, Jennie Vance? I never! What a story!"

"You did, Miss Dimple; you spelt it out
in the Reader, — 'straw-bry;' or I shouldn't
have thought of such a thing."

"Well, I didn't care much about going,
now truly, Jennie; for I don't feel very
well."

"You *seemed* to be very much pleased.
You said, 'How nice!' as much as twice;
and didn't you almost laugh out loud in the
spelling class? Hark! what a clap!"

"I should think you'd be ashamed," said poor Dotty, hopping on one foot. "When I laughed it was to see Charlie Gray make up faces. And should I have gone barefoot if it hadn't been for you?"

"Well, there, Dotty Dimple, you're a smart little girl, I must say! I don't mean to ask you to my party, if my mother lets me have one; and I've a great mind not to speak to you again as long as I live."

"I shouldn't think you'd dare to quarrel, Jennie Vance, when you may die the next minute. Let's get under this tree."

"Lightning strikes trees, you goosie!"

"O, Jennie Vance! isn't there a barn anywhere in this great pasture?"

"Men don't keep barns in their pastures, Dot Dimple; and lightning strikes barns, too, quicker 'n a flash!"

Dotty covered her face with her hands.

"You don't seem to know scarcely anything," continued Jennie, soothingly. "I
don't believe you know what a conductor is."

"Of course I do. It's the man on the
cars that takes your ticket."

"No; that's one kind; but in storms like
this a conductor is a — a conductor is a —
why, I mean if a thing is a conductor, Dotty, — why then the thunder and lightning
conducts it all to pieces, and that's the last
there is of it! My father's got a book of
hijommerty that tells all about such things.
You can't know for certain. Just as likely
as not, now, our baskets are conductors;
and then again perhaps they are *non;* and I
don't know which is the worst. If we were
sure they were *either one,* we ought to throw
'em away! that's a fact!"

"Yes, indeed!" cried Dotty, tossing
hers behind her as if it had been a living

scorpion. "Do you s'pose *hats* will conduct?"

"Nonsense! no. I didn't say baskets
would, did I?" returned Jennie, who still
held her own dangling from her arm.
"Yours was a perfect beauty, Dot. What
a fuss you make!"

As Dotty had all this while been stifling
her groans of pain, and had also been careful not to express a hundredth part of her
real terror of lightning, she thought her
friend's words were, to say the least, a little
severe.

"Why, this is queer," cried Jennie, stop-
ping short. "It's growing wet here; haven't
you noticed it? Now I've thought of something. There's a bog in this town, *somewhere*, so awful and deep that once a boy
slumped into it, don't you think, up to his
waist; and the more he tried to get out the

A Sad Fright.   Page 80.

more he couldn't; and there he was, slump,
slump, and got in as far as his neck. And
he screamed till he was black and blue; and
when they went to him there wasn't a bit of
him out but the end of his nose, and he
couldn't scream any more; so all they could
do was to pull him out by the hair of his
head."

"Is that a true story, now, honest?" cried
Dotty, wringing her hands. "How dreadful, dreadful, dreadful! What shall we do?"

"Do?" was the demure reply; "stand as
stock-still as ever we can, and try not to
shake when we breathe. Next thing we
might slump."

"I do shake," said Dotty; "I can't help it."

"Don't you say anything, Dotty Dimple.
I never should have thought of going across
lots if you hadn't wanted to; and now you'd
better keep still."

6

So even this horrible predicament was owing to Dotty; she was to blame for everything. "Stock-still" they stood under the beating rain, their hearts throbbing harder than the drops.

Yes, there certainly was a bottomless pond — Dotty had heard of it; on its borders grew the pitcher-plant which uncle Henry had brought home once. It was a green pitcher, very pretty, and if it had been glass it could have been set on the table with maple molasses in it (only nobody but poor people used molasses).

O, there *was* a deep, deep pond, and grass grew round it and in it; and uncle Henry had said it was no place for children; they could not be trusted to walk anywhere near it, for one false step might lead them into danger. And now they had come to this very spot, this place of unknown horrors!

What should they do? Should they stand
there and be struck by lightning, or try to
go on, and only sink deeper and deeper till
they choked and drowned?

Never in all Dotty's little life had she
been in such a strait as this. She cried so
loud that her voice was heard above the
storm, in unearthly shrieks. She didn't
want to die! O, it was so nice to be alive!
She would as lief have the sore throat all
the time, if she might only be alive. She
said not a word, but the thoughts flew
through her mind like a flock of startled
swallows, — not one after another, but all
together: and so fast that they almost took
her breath away.

And O, such a naughty girl as she had
been! Going barefoot! Telling a story
about Crossman's orchard! Making believe
she never fibbed, when she did the same

thing as that, and she knew she did. Running off to play when grandma wished her to stay with Flyaway. Feeding Zip Coon with plum cake to see him wag his tail, and never telling but it was brown bread. Getting angry with the chairs and tables, and people. Doing all manner of wickednesses.

Dotty was appalled by the thought of one sin in particular. She remembered that in repeating the Lord's prayer once, she had asked for "daily bread and butter." Her mother had reproved her for it, but she had done the same thing again and again. By and by, when her mother positively forbade her to say "butter," she had said "bread and molasses;" "for, mamma," said she, "you know I don't like *bare* bread."

"I s'pose Miss Preston would say that was the awfulest wickedness of all, and I guess it was. O, dear!"

Well, if she ever got home she would be a better girl. But it wasn't likely she ever should get home.

"Why, Jennie," said she, speaking now for the first time; "here we are; and when we stand still we don't move at all; we don't go home a bit, Jennie."

"Of course not, Dotty Dimple; that's a very bright speech! I've thought the same thought my own self before ever you did!"

Another silence, broken only by the pitter patter of the rain; for the thunder was growing less and less frequent.

"But we must go home some time," cried Jennie with energy. "If it kills us to death we must go home. Just you put your foot out, Dotty dear, and see if it sinks way down, down. I thought it was beginning to grow a little soft right here."

"O, dear, I don't dare to!" groaned Dotty, shaking with a nervous chill; "you put your foot in your own self, Jennie Vance, and see where it goes to. I don't want to slump down up to my hair any more 'n you do. What do you s'pose?"

"Fie! for shame, Dotty Dimple! I always thought you were a coward, and now I know it! What if I should give you my ring, made of all carrot gold, would you do it then? Just nothing but put your foot out?"

"*Would* you give me the ring now, honest?" said Dotty, raising her little foot cautiously; "certain true?"

"Why, you know, Dotty, if I said I would, I would."

A sudden thought was darting across Dotty's mind, like another startled swallow; only this one came alone, and did not take her breath away; for it was a pleasant

thought — Where were they? Whose field
was this?

Why, it was Mr. Gordon's pasture. And
Johnny came here for the cow every night
of his life. And, as true as the world, there
was the Gordon cow now, the red and white
one, standing by the fence, lowing for
Johnny.

"A great deal of a bottomless pond this
is, and so I should think!" said Dotty to
herself, with a smile. "Where a cow can go
I guess I can go with my little feet. Soft?
why, it isn't any softer than anybody's field
is after it rains."

So, without saying a word, the little girl
put her foot out, and of course it touched
solid earth.

"There!" she cried, "I did it, I did it!
You said I was a coward; who's a coward
now? Where's your gold ring, Jennie
Vance?"

"Why, the ground is as hard as a nut, I declare," said Jennie, walking along after Dotty with great satisfaction. "I didn't much think there was a swamp in this field, all the time. Only I thought, if there was, what a scrape it would be! Come to think of it, I believe that bottomless pond is in the town of Augusta."

"No," replied Dotty, "it's on the other side of the river. I know, for uncle Henry went to it in a boat. But where's my ring?"

"I don't know anything about your ring; didn't know you had any."

"I mean *yours*, Jennie Vance; or it *was* yours; the one on your forefinger, with a red stone in it, that you said you'd give to me if I'd put my foot in it."

"Put your foot in what?"

"Why, you know, Jennie Vance; in the mud."

"Well, there wasn't any mud; 'twas as hard as a nut."

"You know what I mean, Jennie," exclaimed Dotty, growing excited. "So you needn't pretend!"

"I'm not pretending, nor any such a thing," replied Jennie, with a great show of candor; "it's you that are making up a story, Dotty Dimple. I didn't say I'd give you my ring. No, ma'am; if 'twas the last words I was to speak, I never!"

"O, Jennie Vance! Jane Sidney Vance! I should think the thunder and lightning would conduct you to pieces this minute; and a bear out of the woods, and every thing else in this world. I never saw a little girl, that had a father named Judge, that would lie so one to another in all the days of my life."

"Well," said Jennie, coolly, "if you've

got done your preaching, I'll tell you what I
said. I said, 'What if I should;' so there!
I didn't say I would, and I never meant to;
and you may ask my father if I can get it
off my finger without sawing the bone in
two."

"Indeed!" replied Dotty, poising her
head backward with queenly dignity; "indeed!"

"I didn't tell a story," said Jennie, uneasily. "I should think any goosie might know
people wouldn't give away jewels just for
putting your foot out."

"It's just as well," said Dotty, with ex-
treme dignity; "just *precisely* as well! I
have one grandmamma who is a Quakeress,
and she don't think much of little girls that
wear rings. Ahem!"

Jennie felt rather uncomfortable. She
did not mind Dotty's anger, but her quiet
contempt was another thing.

"I think likely I may go to Boston next week," said she; "and if I do, this is the last time we shall go strawberrying together this summer."

"O, is it?" said Dotty.

After this the two little creatures trudged on in silence till they reached Mr. Parlin's gate. Jennie ran home in great haste as soon as she was free from her limping companion; and Dotty entered the side-door dripping like a naiad.

"Why, Alice Parlin!" said grandmamma, in dismay; "how came you in such a plight? We never thought of your being out in this shower. We supposed, of course, you would go to Mrs. Gray's, and wait till it was over."

"We were nowhere near Mr. Gray's," faltered Dotty, "nor anywhere else, either."

"I should think you had been standing under a water-spout," said aunt Louise.

"Grandma, can't you put her through the wringer?" asked Prudy, laughing.

Dotty sank in a wet heap on the floor, and held up her ailing foot with a groan.

"Why, child, barefoot?" cried aunt Louise. Dotty said nothing, but frowned with pain.

"It is a cruel thorn," said her good grandmother, putting on her spectacles and surveying the wound.

"Yes, 'm," said Dotty, finding her tongue. "I almost thought 'twould go clear through, and come out at the top of my foot."

Katie took a peep. "No, it didn't," said she; "it hided."

"There, there, poor little dear," said grandmother; "we'll put her right to bed. Ruthie, don't you suppose you and I can carry her up stairs?"

Not a word yet about the naughtiness;

but plenty of pity and soft poultices for
the wounded foot.

"She's a very queer child," thought Ruth,
coming down stairs afterwards to steep hops
for some beer; "a very odd child. She has
something on her mind; but *we* shan't be
any the wiser till she gets ready to tell it."

CHAPTER VI.

MAKING POETRY.

BUT when Prudy had come to bed, Dotty could talk more freely.

"O, dear," said she, hiding her face in her sister's bosom; "I don't want them to laugh at me, but I've lost my boots and my basket, and been dripped in the rain, and got a thorn in my foot too, till it seems as if I should die!"

"But you'll never do so again, little sister," said Prudy, who could think of no other consolation to give.

"And lightning besides, Prudy! And she made me throw away my beautiful picnic basket, and she kept hers, and it never hurt her a bit! Don't you think she was just as mean! What makes grandma let me go with her, do you s'pose? I shall grow real bad! Won't you tell her to stop it?"

Dotty moaned with pain, and between her moans she talked very fast.

"And all this time," said she, "we haven't any ducks!"

Prudy, who was dropping off to sleep, murmured, "No."

"But it's real too bad, Prudy. I never saw such a lazy old hen — did you? Prudy, *did* you?"

Presently, when Prudy thought it must be nearly morning, there was a clutch upon her shoulder, and a voice cried in her ear, —

"I don't see what makes you go to sleep, Prudy Parlin, when my foot aches so bad! And O, how I want a drink o' water!"

Prudy thought she should never find the match-box; but she did at last, and lighted the lamp after several trials. It was dreary work, though, going down stairs with those sticks in her eyes, to get the water.

Dotty drained the nipperkin at two draughts, and said it wasn't half enough.

"O, you shall have all you want, little sister," said Prudy, kindly; "you may drink up the whole barrel if you like."

So down she went again, and this time brought a pitcher. On her return she found Dotty weeping in high displeasure.

"You told me to drink up that whole barrel, you did," cried the unreasonable child, shaking her head.

"Did I?" said Prudy; "well, dear, I didn't mean anything."

"But you *said* so — the whole, whole barrel," repeated Dotty, rocking back and

forth; "you talk to me just as if I—was
—black!"

"Hush!" said Prudy, "or you'll wake
grandma. Let me see; do you want me to
tell you a conundrum? Why does an elephant carry his trunk?"

"I don't know; I s'pose he can't help it;
it grows on the end of his nose."

"That isn't the answer, though, Dotty;
it's because—because he's a traveller!"

"An elephant a traveller? Where does
he travel to? I don't believe it."

"Well," replied Prudy, "I can't see any
sense in it myself. O, stop a minute! Now
I know; I didn't tell it right. This is the
way: 'Why is an elephant like a traveller?
Because he carries a trunk?' Isn't that
funny?"

"I don't care anything about your ele-
phants," said Dotty· "if you don't try to

please me, Prudy Parlin, you'll have to wake
up grandma, and call her in here, or I shall
cry myself sick ! "

Patient Prudy crept into bed, but left the
lamp burning.

"Suppose we make up some poetry?" said
she.

"Why, you don't know how to make up poetry — do you?" said Dotty, leaning on her
elbow, and looking with dreamy eyes at the
engraving of Christus Consolator at the foot
of the bed. "I love poetry when they read
it in concert at school. Don't you know, —

'Tremendous torrents! For an instant hush!'

Isn't that splendid?"

"Very splendid, indeed," replied Prudy,
pinching herself to keep awake.

"I think Torrence is *such* a nice name,"
pursued Dotty; "don't you tell anybody,

but when I'm married and have some boys,
I'm going to name some of them Torrence."

"Not more than one, Dotty!"

"O, no, I couldn't; could I? There mustn't
but one of them have the same name; I forgot. 'Tremendous Torrence!' I shall say;
and then he'll come in and ask, 'What do
you want, mother?'"

Prudy suddenly hid her face under the
sheet. The absurdity of little Dotty's ideas
had driven the sleep out of her eyes.

"It would do very well for a name for a
very queer boy," said she, stifling a laugh;
"but a torrent *generally* means the Niagara
Falls."

"Does it?" said Dotty; "who told you so?
But I guess I shall call him by it just the
same though — if his father is willing."

Dotty looked very much interested.

"What will you call the rest of your

boys?" asked Prudy, glad to talk of anything which kept her little sister pleasant.

"I shan't have but two boys, and I shall
name the other one for his father," replied
Dotty, thoughtfully; "I shall have eight
girls, for I like girls very much; and I
shall dress them in silk and velvet, with
gold rings on all their fingers, a great deal
handsomer than Jennie Vance's; but they
won't be proud a bit. They never will have
to be punished; for when they do wrong I
shall look through my spectacles and say,
'Why, my eight daughters, I'm very much
surprised!' And then they will obey me in
a minute."

"Yes," returned Prudy; "but don't you
think now we'd better go to sleep?"

"No, indeed," said Dotty, drawing herself up in a little heap and holding her
throbbing foot in her hand; "if you don't

make poetry I'm going to make it myself.
Hark !——

'Once there was a little boy going down hill;
  He leaped, he foamed, he struggled; — and all was o'er.'"

"Do you call that poetry?" said Prudy,
laughing. "Why, where's the rhyme?"

"The rhyme? I s'pose I forgot to put it
in. Tell me what a rhyme is, Prudy; *maybe*
I don't know!"

"A rhyme," replied her wise sister, "is a
jingle like this : 'A boy and a toy,' 'A goose
and a moose.'"

"O, is it? how queer! 'A hill and a pill,'
that's a rhyme, too."

"Now," continued Prudy, "I'll make up
some real poetry, and show you how. It
won't take me more than a minute; it's just
as easy as knitting-work."

Prudy thought for a few seconds, and then

recited the following lines in a sing-song
tone : —

> "When the sun
> Had got his day's work done,
> He put a red silk cloud on his head,
>   (*For a night-cap, you know,*)
> And went to bed.
> He was there all sole alone;
> For just at that very time the moon
> (*That isn't a very nice rhyme, but I can't help it*)
> Was dressed and up,
> And had eaten her sup-
> Per. 'Husband,' said Mrs. Moon, 'I can't
>   stop to kiss you good by;
> I've got to leave you now and go up in
>   the sky.'"

"O, how pretty!" said Dotty; "how it
jingles! Did you make it up in your own
head?"

"Yes, indeed; just as fast as I could knit
once round. I could do a great deal better
if I should spend more time. I mean to
take a slate some time and write it all
full of stars, and clouds, and everything

splendid. I shall say, ' What a pity it is that
a nice husband and wife, like the sun and
moon, can't ever live together, but have to
keep following each other round the sky and
never get near enough to shake hands!' I'll
pretend that it makes the moon look very
sober indeed, but the sun isn't so tender-
hearted; so he can bear it better. O, Dotty, don't you let me forget to put that into
poetry! I can jingle it off, and make it
sound beautiful!"

"I should think you might put my verse
into poetry, too. Can't you say 'a pill rolled
down hill'?" said Dotty.

"O, I can make poetry of it easier than
that. You don't need to change but one
word :—

> 'There was a little boy going down hill,
>   He leaped, he foamed, he struggled;—and all
>   was *still*.'"

Dotty repeated it several times with much delight. "That's beautiful," said she, "now honest; and I did almost the whole of it myself!"

After this she began to grow drowsy, and, forgetting her troubles, fell asleep, to the great relief of poor sister Prudy, who was not long in following her.

Next morning Prudy awoke at nearly the usual time; but her sister was still in the land of dreams, and she stole out of the room without disturbing her.

"Grandmamma," said she, "Dotty has had an awful night! I've had to be up with her, and trying to pacify her, most of the time."

"A whole hour," said grandma, smiling.

"O, grandma, it was nearly all night, but there didn't anybody know it; we talked low, so we needn't disturb you."

Grandmother and aunt Maria smiled at each other across the table.

"I dare say, my dear," said aunt Maria, "you thought you were as quiet as two little mice; but I assure you, you kept everybody awake, except grandpa and Susy."

"Why, aunt 'Ria!"

"But we learned a lesson in poetry-making," said aunt Louise, "which was worth lying awake to hear. Don't you suppose, Maria, that even prosy people, like you and me, might jingle poetry till in time it would become as easy as knitting-work?"

Prudy blushed painfully.

"I thought," said Grace, "the sun must look very jolly in his red silk night-cap, only I was sorry you forgot to tell what he had for breakfast."

"Nothing but cold potatoes out of the cupboard," said Horace; "he keeps bachelor's hall. It's just as well the old fellow can't meet his wife, for she's made of green cheese, and he'd be likely to slice her up and eat her."

A tear glittered on Prudy's eyelashes. Horace was the first to observe it, and he hastened to change the subject by saying his johnny-cake was so thin he could cut it with a pair of scissors.· By that time Prudy's tears had slyly dropped upon her napkin, and she would have recovered her spirits if aunt Louise had not remarked carelessly,—

"Seems to me our little poetess is rather melancholy this morning."

Prudy's heart was swollen so high with tears that there would have been a flood in about a minute; but Horace exclaimed suddenly,—

"O, mother, may I tell a story? Once there were two old—two maiden ladies in Nantucket, and they earned their living by going round the island picking up the 'tag-locks' the sheep had left hanging to the bushes and rocks. Now, you wouldn't believe, would you, mother, that those two women could get rich by selling tag-locks?"

"I certainly should not," replied Mrs. Clifford, smiling fondly on her young son; for she saw and approved of his kind little scheme for diverting his cousin's attention.

"Well, mother, they lived to be more than sixty years old; and when they made their wills, how much money do you suppose they had to leave? I wish you'd try to guess."

"Dear me," said Mrs. Clifford, "I'm sure I can't imagine: I shall have to give it up."

"So must I," said grandmamma; "I make such poor work at guessing: I suppose they lived very frugally?"

"A thousand dollars?" suggested Grace.

"A million?" said Susy.

"A shilling?" chimed in aunt Louise.

" *Not one cent!* " replied Horace.

"Well, well," said grandmother, "you've caught us napping this time."

But only she and aunt Maria appreciated Horace's gallantry towards his sensitive cousin Prudy.

CHAPTER VII.

A DAY ON THE SOFA.

WHEN Dotty Dimple awoke that morning, she was very much astonished to see the sun so high.

"The sky looks very clean," said she, "and I should think it might after such a washing."

She did not know it, but for some reason the pure blue of the heavens made her feel dissatisfied with herself. Since she had slept upon it, her last night's conduct seemed worse to her than ever. All this while her grandmamma's forgiveness had not been asked. Must it be asked? Dotty hung her proud head for shame. Then she offered her morning prayer, and promised God that henceforth she would try to be good.

"If Jennie Vance only stays away," added she, meekly.

The fact was, Dotty was losing faith in herself. She had boasted that she never told a lie; she had "preached" to Jennie Vance; and now, behold, what had she been doing herself! The child was full of good resolutions to-day, but she began to find that her strongest purposes did not hold together any longer than her gingham dresses.

Her foot was so lame and swollen that she made believe the staircase was a hill, and slid down it accordingly. As she hobbled by the parlor door, she saw her aunt Maria seated on the sofa sewing. It must be very late, she knew. Little Flyaway, who had been chasing the cat, ran to meet her, look-

ing very joyful because her cousin had over-
slept herself.

"It's half past o'clock," said she, clapping
her little hands; "half past o'clock, Dotty
Dimple!"

Dotty felt quite ashamed, but her grandmother assured her that although it was
nearly ten o'clock, she was perfectly excu-
sable. She seated her in an easy chair, and
gave her a cracker to nibble; for Dotty said
she was not hungry, and did not care for
breakfast.

There was one thought uppermost in the
little girl's mind: she must ask her grandmother's forgiveness. Some children might
not have seen the necessity, but Dotty had
been well instructed at home; she knew this
good, kind grandmamma was deserving of
the highest respect, and if any of her grand-
children disobeyed her, they could do no less

than acknowledge their fault. But Dotty was a very proud child; she could not humble herself yet.

Mrs. Parlin dressed the lame foot, and pitied it, and was very sorry the little girl had any soreness of the throat; but not a word of reproach did she utter; she was waiting to see if Dotty had anything to say for herself.

Susy and Prudy had gone to aunt Martha's; and till "the Charlie boy" came, there was no one at home for company but little Katie. Dotty did not wish to think; so she made the best of the little ones, and played "keep school."

Black Dinah was the finest-looking pupil, but there were several others made of old shawls and table-covers, who sat bolt upright, and bore their frequent whippings very meekly. Katie and Charlie each held

a birch switch, and took the government of
the school, while Dotty did the teaching.

"Spell *man*," said Dotty, sternly, pointing
with a bodkin at Dinah.

Dinah was sulky, and kept her red silk
mouth shut; but Dotty answered for her:
"m, a, n, man."

"To," said she to the black and white
shawl: "t, ò, to." "Put," to the green
table-cover: "p, u, t, put."

"We 'shamed o' you," said Katie, beating
the whole school unmercifully. "Why don't
you mind in a minute? Let *me* spell 'em!
Hush, Dinah! Say put! T, o, put!"

"I think," said Dotty, laughing, "it is
time now for Dinah to take her music lesson."

"Yes," said Katie, "lady wants um to
packus."

So the colored miss was set on the music

8

stool, and both her kid hands spread out
upon the keys.

"Don't um packus booful?" said Katie,
admiringly.

But next moment Charlie was punishing
the pupil because she didn't "breeve."
"Lady wanth her to breeve when her
packithith."

As it was an ingrain misfortune of Dinah's that she could not breathe, she showed
no signs of repentance.

"Stop!" said Dotty; "she looks faint;
it is rheumatism, I think."

"O, O, roosum-tizzum! Poo' Dinah!"
said Katie.

"We must pack her in a wet sheet," said
Dotty.

Katie was sent to the kitchen for a towel
and a basin of water; and very soon Dinah's
clothes were removed, and she was rolled up

in a pack ; like the boy in the swamp, with
"not a bit of her out but the end of her
nose."

"Ow ! Ow !" cried Katie, in a tone of
agony, speaking for Dinah. "Ow ! O,
dear ! "

This was what the black patient would
have said, no doubt, if she had had her
faculties. Aunt Maria came in, a little
alarmed, to inquire what was the matter
with Katie.

"Nuffin, mamma, only we *suffer* Dinah,"
replied the child, dancing round the patient ;
"her wants to ky, but her can't. · Gets
caught in her teef comin' out ! "

"Very well," said Mrs. Clifford, kissing
the small nurse, " you may ' suffer' Dinah as
much as you like, but please don't scream
quite so loud."

"Is grandma busy, aunt 'Ria ? " said Dot-

ty; "because I'd like to see her a moment."

The child had seized her knitting-work.
Her face was flushed and eager. She thought
she felt brave enough to open her heart to
her grandmother; but when Mrs. Parlin entered the nursery, her face beaming with
kindness, Dotty was not ready.

"O, grandma," stammered she, "are there
any ducks hatched? Don't you think that
hen is very slow and very lazy?"

Mrs. Parlin knew her little granddaughter
had not called her out of the kitchen merely
to ask about the poultry. She seated herself on the sofa, and drew Dotty's head into
her lap.

"Please look at my knitting-work, grandma. Shall I seam that stitch or *plain*
it?"

"You are doing very well," said Mrs. Par-

lin, looking at the work; "you seamed in
the right place."

Dotty cast about in her mind for something more to say.

"Grandma, you know what fireflies are?
Well, if you scratch 'em will they light a
lamp? Susy says they have *fosfos* under
their wings, like a match."

"No, Alice ; with all the scratching in
the world, they could not be made to light
a lamp."

Dotty sighed.

"Grandma, there are some things in this
world I hate, and one is skeetos."

"They are vexatious little creatures, it is
true."

There was a long pause.

"Grandma, are skeetos idiotic ? You
said people without brains were idiotic, and
there isn't any place in a skeeto's head
for brains."

"Dotty," said grandma, rising with a smile, "if you sent for me to ask me such foolish questions as these, I must really beg to be excused. I have a pudding to make for dinner."

"Grandma, O, grandma," cried Dotty, seizing her skirts, "I have something to say, now truly; something real sober. I — I —"

"Well, my dear," said Mrs. Parlin, encouragingly.

"I — I — O, grandma, which do you think can knit the best, Prudy or I?"

"My dear Dotty," said the kind grandmother, stroking the child's hair, "don't be afraid to tell me the whole story. I know you have a trouble at your heart. Do you think you were a naughty girl last night?"

Dotty's head drooped. She tried to say,

"Yes, ma'am;" but, like Dinah, "the words got caught in her teef comin' out."

"We didn't go where you thought we did, grandma," faltered she at last. "Mr. Crossman has two orchards, and we went to just the one you wouldn't have s'posed."

"Yes, dear; so I have learned to-day."

"I deceived you a-purpose, grandma; for if I hadn't deceived you, you wouldn't have let me go."

There was a sorrowful expression on Mrs. Parlin's face as she listened to these words, though they told her nothing new.

"Has you got a pain, gamma?" said little Katie, tenderly.

"I did another wickedness, grandma," said Dotty in a low voice; "I went barefoot, and you never said I might."

"Poor little one, you were sorely punished for that," said grandma, kindly.

"And another too I did; I threw my basket away; but that wasn't much wicked; Jennie made me think perhaps 'twas a non."

"A what?"

"A *non*, that catches lightning, you know; so I threw it away to save my life."

Grandma smiled.

"And now," continued Dotty, twirling her fingers, "can you — can you — forgive me, grandma?"

"Indeed, I can, and will, child, if you are truly sorry."

"There, now, grandma," said Dotty, looking distressed, "you think I don't feel sorry because I don't cry. I can't cry as much as Prudy does, ever; and besides, I cried all my tears away last night."

Dotty rubbed her eyes vigorously as she spoke, but no "happy mist" came over them.

"Why, my dear little Alice," said grand-mamma, "it is quite unnecessary for you to rub your eyes. Don't you know you can *prove* to me that you are sorry?"

"How, grandma?"

"Never do any of these naughty things again. That is the way I shall know that you really repent. Sometimes children think they are sorry, and make a great parade, but forget it next day, and repeat the offence."

"Indeed, grandma, I don't mean ever to deceive or disobey again," said Dotty, with a great deal more than her usual humility.

"Ask your heavenly Father to help you keep that promise," said Mrs. Parlin, solemnly.

CHAPTER VIII.

WASHING THE PIG.

AFTER her grandmother had left the room, Miss Dotty lay on the sofa for five minutes, thinking.

"Then it doesn't make any difference how much anybody cries, or how much they don't cry. If they are truly sorry, then they won't do it again; that's all."

Then she wondered if Jenny Vance had asked her step-mother's pardon. She thought she ought to talk to Jennie, and tell her how much happier she would feel if she would only try to be a good little girl.

"That child is growing naughty every day

of her life," mused Miss Dimple, with a feeling of pity.

There was plenty of time to learn the morning's lesson by heart, for Dotty was obliged to keep very quiet all day. The thorn had been removed from her foot, but the healing must be a work of time; and more than that, her throat was quite sore.

It seemed as if Susy and Prudy would never come; and when at last their cheerful voices were heard ringing through the house, it was a welcome sound indeed. They had brought some oranges for Katie and Dotty, with sundry other niceties, from aunt Martha's.

"Did you know," said Dotty, "I haven't had any breakfast to-day? I've lost one meal, and I never shall make it up as long as I live; for I couldn't eat two breakfasts, you know."

"I'll tell you what we'll do," said aunt Louise, laughing; "if you'll wake me up at twelve o'clock some night, I'll rise and prepare a breakfast for you, and that will make it all right."

Dotty looked at her auntie as if she did not know whether to take her in earnest or not.

"I've been sick at home all day, Prudy," said she; "and I s'pose *you've* been having a good time."

"Splendid! And Lightning Dodger brought us home."

"Who's Lightning Dodger?"

"Why, aunt Martha's horse; don't you know? They call him that because they say he goes so fast the lightning don't have time to hit him."

"O, you don't believe it — do you?" cried Dotty; "I guess that's poetry."

"Little sister," replied Prudy, speaking in a low voice, "don't say 'poetry' ever again. There's something about it that's very queer. I thought I knew how to make poetry, but they all laugh at me, even grandma."

Dotty looked greatly surprised.

"Yes," continued Prudy, with a trembling voice; "I can rhyme verses and jingle them; but there's something else I don't put in, I s'pose, that belongs there. Some time I'll look in the big dictionary and see what it is."

"Is Prudy telling about the party?" asked Susy, from the corner.

"What party?" cried Dotty, dancing on her well foot.

"There, now, don't feel so happy, darling, for you can't go; it's a family party, and cousin Lydia wrote she hadn't room for the two youngest; that's you and Flyaway."

Dotty looked as if she had received a blow. True, she knew nothing about cousin Lydia, who lived twenty miles away; but if that individual was going to have a party, of course Dotty wished to go to it.

"Uncle John is going, and all *his* wife and children," said Prudy; "and I don't see why Dotty can't."

Uncle John was aunt Martha's husband; and "all *his* wife and children" meant only aunt Martha and Lonnie.

"Cousin Lydia wanted to make me cry!" exclaimed Dotty, her eyes shooting out sparks of displeasure; "she 'spected I'd cry, and that's why — Katie," added she, drawing the little one up to her, "cousin Lydia won't let you come to her house."

"What *for* she won't?" cried Katie, looking defiant. "If I goed would her put me in the closet? I don't like her tall, tenny rate."

This was the strongest expression of wrath Katie dared use; and when she said she did not like a person "tall tenny rate," it meant that she was very, very angry.

"Has cousin Yiddy got some heart?" asked she, indignantly.

"Not a bit," replied Dotty, fiercely.

Mrs. Parlin now tried to explain. She said Mrs. Tenney did not intend any disrespect to the two youngest ones; but she really had no room for them, as her guests were to spend the night.

"The mistake she made was in asking Susy and Prudy," said aunt Louise; "but I suppose she was curious to see our little poetess."

Prudy blushed, and hid her face behind the curtain.

"Poor little sister," thought she, "how she feels!" For Dotty sat in the rocking-

chair, as stiff as a jointed doll, looking as if
she loved nobody and nobody loved her.
Her beautiful eyes had ceased to shoot
sparks of fire, and now appeared hard and
frozen, like thick blue ice. In fact, a fit of
the pouts was coming on very fast, and gentle Prudy dreaded it. She has been so happy in the thought of riding to Bloomingdale;
could she give up that pleasure, and stay at
home with Dotty? Nothing less, she knew,
would satisfy the child. All her life Prudy
had been learning to think of the happiness
of others before her own. She cast another
glance at the still face.

"I'm not going to Bloomingdale," sighed
she behind the curtain.

But when she told Mrs. Parlin so, that
night, her voice was very tremulous.

"You dear little girl," said grandma, giving her a hearty kiss; "you need not make

any such resolve. Your sister Alice must
learn to bear disappointments as well as you.
You are going to Bloomingdale with us, my
child; so bring your blue dress to me, and
let me see if it is in order."

Though Prudy's offer to remain at home
had been made in all good faith, and though
she was really sorry to think of leaving
Dotty alone, still I cannot say her heart did
not bound with delight on being told she
must go.

Thursday morning came clear and bright,
and with it Miss Polly, downcast and sad, in
a mournful brown bonnet, the front of
which, as Prudy said, was "making a courte-
sy." Miss Polly was, however, in as good
spirits as usual, and had come to keep house
with Ruth, and help take care of the children for this day and the next.

Till the last minute Prudy and Dotty

9

walked the piazza, their arms about each
other's waist.

"I s'pose," said Dotty, sullenly, "when
you are at that old cousin Lydia's, having
good times, you won't think anything about
me and Katie, left here all alone."

"Why, little sister!"

"Maybe," continued Dotty, "the ducks
will hatch while you're gone. I saw the
white hen flying over the fence with one of
those eggs in her mouth."

"A piece of the shell?"

"O, no, a whole egg, right in her bill,"
replied Dotty, who supposed she was telling
the truth. "And you know those big strawberries that cost a cent apiece, Prudy; you'll
be sorry you couldn't be here to help eat
'em in cream."

Perhaps Dotty hoped, even at this last
moment, that Prudy would be induced to

stay at home. If so, she was doomed to be disappointed.

"Well," said Prudy, "I'm glad you'll have such nice times, Dotty."

"O, it won't be nice at all. Something will happen; now you see if it don't," said Dotty, determined to be miserable.

After the two carriages, with the horses "Deacon" and "Judge," had driven off, and grandpa had given his last warning about fire, and Horace and the girls had waved their handkerchiefs for the last time, Dotty proceeded to the kitchen to see if she could find anything wherewith to make herself unhappy. Ruth stood by the flour-board kneading bread, and cutting it with a chopping-knife in a brisk, lively way. Polly sat by the stove sighing and rubbing silver.

"Dear me, child, what are you doing with my starch?" said Ruth as she saw

Dotty with the bowl at her lips, and a sticky stream trickling down her apron.

"Starch?" cried Dotty in disgust; "and you never told me, Ruthie! How did I know it wasn't arrow-root?"

"You see, Polly," said Ruth in a discouraged tone, "just what we are to expect from these children to-day. Next thing we know, that morsel of a Katie will be running away. They are enough to try the patience of Job when they both of them set out to see what they *can* do. And if Jennie Vance comes, the house will be turned upside down in five minutes."

Ruth might have known better than to complain to Polly, who always had something in her own experience which was worse than anybody else had known.

"We all have our trials," sighed that sorrowful woman; "if it isn't children, it's aches and pains.   Now, for my part, I've been troubled for ten years with—"

Here followed a list of diseases. Ruth shut her lips together, resolved to say nothing more about her own trials.

"They don't either of them like me," thought Dotty. "I'm going off in the barn, and perhaps they'll think I'm dead. Katie," said she, sternly, "I'm going off somewhere, and you must n't try to find me."

Then there was some one else who felt quite alone in the world, and that was little Katie. Her cousin had pushed her one side as if she was of no value. Katie was a very little child, but she was old enough to feel aggrieved. She went into the parlor, and threw herself face downwards on the sofa, thinking.

"Somebody leave me alone. O, dear! Some naughty folks don't think I'm any gooder than a baby."

Then the poor little thing ran out to "breve the fleshy air." No, she wasn't quite alone in the world after all, for there was Charlie Gray at the gate.

"Is um *you?*" she cried gleefully.

Charlie said it was.

"You didn't came to see big folks — did you? You camed to see Katie. I love you decly."

Then she tried to kiss him; but Charlie drew away.

"O, is your face sore?" asked the little girl.

By this time they had got as far as the seat in the trees, and Charlie had found his tongue.

"I didn't come thee *you*," said he. "I came thee your grandpa'th pig."

"O," said Katie, perfectly satisfied.

Off they started for the pig-pen.

"I'm glad Dotty Dimble goed away," said Katie, swinging Charlie's hand; "her's stinchy and foolidge."

"Good girlth don't thay tho," said sweet little Charlie, rather shocked.

"Well, I do; stinchy and foolidge!" repeated Katie, as severely as if she had known what the words meant.

The pig was not expecting any visitors, and when he found that Charlie and Katie had brought him nothing to eat, he did not seem very glad to see them.

"How you do, piggy?" said Katie, swinging a stick through the opening by the trough.

Piggy ran away, looking very unamiable; and then he came back again, rolling his little eyes, and grunting sulkily.

"He don't look pleathant," said Charlie.

"No," replied Katie, archly; "I guess um don't want to be kissed."

Piggy winked his pink eyes, as if to say,
"Ah, but I do."

"Does you?" said Katie, kindly; "then
I'll frow you one;" and she did it from the
tips of her clean fingers.

"But piggy's velly dirty," said she, wiping her lips on her apron.

"Don't they wath him?" said Charlie;
"they wath theep."

"Um isn't a sheep," returned Katie;
"um's a pig."

"But your gwampa could wath him."

"No, gampa couldn't; gampa's deaf. I'll
tell Ruthie, and Ruthie 'll wash him with the
toof-brush."

"I with thee would," sighed Charlie; "thee
ought to. O ho!" he added, a bright thought
striking him; "you got a mop?"

"A mop?"

"Yes; a bwoom 'thout any bwoom on it;
only wags."

Katie knew what he meant in a minute; and soon her hair was flying in the wind, as she ran into the house for the handled mop. She looked first in the parlor, and then in the front hall; but at last she found it in the wash-room. She was very sly about it, for she was not sure Ruthie would approve of this kind of housework. Then Charlie tugged out a pail of water, and dipped in the mop; and between them both they thrust it through the opening of the pen, upon piggy's back. But the dirty creature did not love clean water. When he felt the mop coming down, he thought the sky was falling, and ran as fast as Chicken Little frightened by the rose-leaf.

It was of no use. The mop was wilful, and fell into the trough; and there it staid, though the children spent the rest of the forenoon in vain attempts to hook it out.

When Ruthie went that noon to feed the pig,
she found the trough choked with a mop, a
hoe, a shovel, and several clothes-pins. She
did not stop to inquire into the matter, but
took the articles out, one by one, saying to
herself, with a smile, —

"Some of that baby's work. I couldn't
think what had become of my mop; she's
enough to try the patience of Job. And
now," added Ruth, throwing her apron over
her head, "I may as well look up Miss Dimple. There's not a better child in the world
than she is when she pleases; but deary me,
when things do go wrong!"

Just then a wagon drove up to the gate,
and Ruth said, as she saw a burly figure
alight from it, —

"Why, that can't be uncle Seth? I'm
afraid something has happened at our
house!"

CHAPTER IX.

A DARK DAY.

MEANWHILE Dotty was lying on the hay in the barn scaffold. It is very easy to be unhappy when we particularly try to be so; and Dotty had arrived at the point of *almost* believing that she *almost* wished she was actually dead.

And, to add to her gloom, a fierce-looking man, with a long horse-whip in his hand, came and peeped in at the barn door, and screamed to Dotty in a hoarse voice that " Ruth Dillon wanted her right off, and none of her dilly-dallying."

And then, on going into the house, what

should she learn but that this man had come
to take Ruth home, because her mother was
sick. The children — so Ruth said — must
stay with Polly and be little ladies.

O, dear, it was as lonesome as a line-storm,
after lively Ruth had gone away. Dotty
began to think she liked her brisk little
scoldings, after all.

"Does you feel so bad?" said little Flyaway, gazing on her sober cousin with pity;
"your mouth looks juts this way;" and,
putting up both hands, she drew down her
own little lips at the corners.

"Yes, I feel bad," said Dotty. "You
needn't talk to me; where's your orange?"

"I squoze it," replied Flyaway; "and falled
it down my froat. But I didn't had enough.
If you pees, um, give me some more."

"Why, what an idea!" said Dotty,
laughing.

But when she began to divide her own orange into sections, Katie looked on expectantly, knowing she should have a share. Dotty ate two quarters, gave one to Katie, and reserved the fourth for Polly. She longed to eat this last morsel herself, but Polly had praised her once for giving away some toys, and she wished to hear her say again, "Why, what a generous little girl!"

But when she smilingly offered the bite, what was her surprise to hear Polly say in an indifferent tone, —

"Well, well, child, you needn't have saved such a tiny piece for me; it doesn't amount to anything!"

At the same time she ate the whole at a mouthful. Dotty felt very much irritated. Did Miss Polly think oranges grew on bushes? What was the use to be generous if people wouldn't say 'thank you'?

"I don't feel much better than I did when I gave the beggar my money. But I didn't do my 'alms before men' this time, though," said she, looking at her little fat arms and wondering what her grandmother meant by talking of her giving *them* away.

"I s'pose it's my *fingers* that grow on the ends of my arms, and that's what I give with," she concluded.

On the whole she was passing a dismal day. She had been told that she must not go away; and it happened that nobody came, not even Jennie Vance.

"If Prudy had been left alone, all the girls in town would have come to see her," thought the forlorn Miss Dimple, putting a string round one of her front teeth, and trying to pull it out by way of amusement.

"O, dear, I can't move my tooth one inch. If I could get it out, and not put my tongue in the hole, then there'd be a gold one come. But I can't. O, dear!"

"Where is your little cousin?" said Miss Polly, coming into the room with her knitting in her hand. "I thought she was with you: I don't wonder they call her Flyaway."

"I don't know where she is, I'm sure, Miss Polly. Won't you please pull my tooth! And do you 'spose I can keep my tongue out of the hole?"

"Why, Dotty, I thought you were going to take care of that child," said Miss Polly, dropping her knitting without getting around to the seam-needle, and walking away faster than her usual slow pace.

"There's nothing so bad for me as worry of mind: I shall be sick as sure as this world!"

Dotty knew she had been selfish and

careless. She not only felt ashamed of herself, but also very much afraid that something dreadful had happened to Katie, in which case she would be greatly to blame. She anxiously joined in the search for the missing child. I am sure you would never guess where she was found. In the watering trough! Not drowned, because the water was not deep enough.

"I was trying to srim," said she, as they drew her out; "and THAT's what is it."

Even Miss Polly smiled at the dripping little figure with hair clinging close to its head; but Flyaway looked very solemn.

"It makes me povokin'," said she, knitting her brows, "to have you laugh to me!"

"It would look well in you, Dotty," said Miss Polly, "to pay more attention to this baby, and let your teeth alone."

Dotty twisted a lock of her front hair,

and said nothing; but she remembered her grandmother's last words, — "Alice, I depend upon you to amuse your little cousin, as your aunt Maria told you. You know you can make her very happy when you please."

"Seems to me," thought Dotty, "that baby might grow faster and have more sense. *I* never got into a watering-trough in my life! — Why, how dark it is! Hark!" said she, aloud; "what is that rattling against the windows?"

For she heard

> "the driving hail
> Upon the window beat with icy flail."

"That is hail," replied Polly — "frozen drops of rain."

"Why, Miss Polly," said Dotty, giving a fierce twitch at her tooth, "rain can't freeze the least speck in the summer. You don't

10

mean to tell a wrong story, but you've made a mistake."

"Her's made a 'stake," said Katie.

"Now, look, Polly, it's stones! They're pattering, clickety-click, all over the yard. Dear, dear! The grass will look just like the gravel-path, and the windows will crack in two."

"Never you mind," said Polly, knitting as usual; "if it does any harm, 'twill only kill a few chickens."

Upon this there was another wail; for next to ducks Dotty loved chickens. But lo! before her tears had rolled down to meet her dimples, the patter of hail was over.

"Come and see the rainbow," said Polly from the door-stone.

It was a glorious sight, an arch of varied splendor resting against the blue sky.

"That isn't a rainbow," said Dotty; "it's a hail-bow!"

"What a big, big, big bubbil!" shouted Katie.

"She thinks somebody is blowing all that out of soapsuds, I s'pose," said Dotty; "I guess 'twould take a giant with a 'normous pipe — don't you, Polly?"

"There, now," said Miss Polly, "I just want you to hold some of this hail in your hand. What do you call that but ice?"

"So it is," said Dotty; "cold lumps of frozen ice, as true as this world."

"And not stones," returned Polly. "Now you won't think next time you know so much better than older people — will you?"

"But I don't see, Miss Polly, how it got here from Greenland; I don't, now honest."

"I didn't say anything about Greenland,

child. I said it was rain, and it froze in
the air coming down; and so it did."

"Did it? Why, you know a great deal
— don't you, Miss Polly? Did you ever go
to school?"

Polly sighed dismally.

"O, yes, I went now and then a day. I
was what is called a 'bound girl.' I didn't
have nice, easy times, like you little ones.
You have no idea of my hardships. It was
delve and dig from sunrise to sunset."

"Why, what a naughty mother to make
you dig! Did you have a ladies' hoe?"

"My mother died, Dotty, when I was a
creeping baby. The woman who took me
to bring up was a hard-faced woman. She
made me work like a slave."

"Did she? But by and by you grew up,
Miss Polly, and, when you had a husband,
he didn't make you dig — did he?"

"I never had a husband or anybody else to take care of me," said Polly. "Come, children, we must go into the house."

They all three entered the parlor, and Miss Whiting fastened the window tightly to exclude the air, for it was one of her afflictions that she was "easy to take cold."

"I don't see," queried Dotty, "why your husband didn't marry you. I should have thought he would."

"He didn't want to, I suppose," said Polly, grimly.

Dotty fell into a brown study. It was certainly very unkind in *some* man that he hadn't married Miss Polly and taken care of her, so she need not have wandered around the world with a double-covered basket and a snuff-box. It was a great pity; still Dotty could not see that just now it had anything to do with Polly's forgetting to set the table.

"I'm so hungry," said she; "isn't it 'most supper time?"

"It's only five; but you appear to be so lonesome that I'll make a fire this minute and put on the tea-kettle," replied the kind-hearted Polly. "What does your grandmother generally have for supper?"

"Cake sometimes," answered Dotty, her eyes brightening; "and tarts."

"And perjerves," added Katie; "and — and — yice puddin'."

"She keeps the cake in a stone jar," said Dotty, eagerly; "and the strawberries are down cellar in a glass dish — cost a cent apiece."

"The slips they grew from cost a cent apiece; that is what you mean," said Polly; "you hear things rather hap-hazard sometimes, Dotty, and you ought to be more careful."

The tea-kettle was soon singing on the stove, and Dotty forgot her peculiar trials when she saw the table covered with dainties. She was not sure grandma would have approved of the cake and tarts, but they were certainly very nice, and it was a pleasure to see how Polly enjoyed them. Dotty presumed she had never had such things when she lived with the "hard-faced woman."

"It wasn't everywhere," she said, "that she saw such thick cream as rose to the tops of Mrs. Parlin's pans."

She poured it freely over the strawberries and into her own tea, which it made so delicious that she drank three cups. Then after supper she seemed to feel quite cheery for her, and, taking Katie in her arms, rocked her to sleep to the tune of "China," which is not very lively music, it must be confessed.

"Aunt 'Ria puts her to bed awake," said Dotty. "She's going to sleep in my bed to-night."

"Very well," said Polly, "but you will sleep with me."

"Why, Miss Polly! what if Katie should wake up?"

"She won't be likely to; but I can't help it if she does. I may have the nightmare in the night."

"What is the nightmare?"

"It is something perfectly dreadful, child! I sincerely hope you'll never know by sad experience. It's the most like dying of any feeling I ever had in my life. I can't move a finger, but if I don't move it's sure death; and somebody has to shake me to bring me out of it."

Dotty turned pale.

"Miss Polly, O, please, I'd rather sleep with Katie!"

"But how would you feel to have me die
in the night?"

"O, dear, dear, dear," cried Dotty; "let
me go for the doctor this minute!"

"Why, child, I haven't got it now, and
perhaps I shan't have it at all; but if I do,
I shall groan, and that's the way you will
know."

Dotty ran into the shed, threw her apron,
still sticky with starch, over her head, and
screamed at the wood-pile.

"O, if grandma were only at home, or
Ruth, or Abner!"

"Why, what's the matter, little Goody-
Two-Shoes?" said a manly voice. Abner
had just come from his day's work in the
meadow.

"Polly's here," gasped Dotty. "She's
afraid she's going to die in the night, and
she wants me to shake her."

Abner leaaed against a beam, and laughed heartily.

"Never you fear, little one! I have heard that story about Polly's dying in the night ever since I can remember; and she hasn't died yet. You just say your prayers, dear, and go to sleep like a good little girl, and that's the last you'll know about it till morning.".

So saying, he caught Dotty by the shoulders, and tossed her up to the rafters. The child's spirits rose at once. It was such a comfort to have that strong Abner in the house in case of accidents.

She said her prayers more earnestly than usual, but it was nearly five minutes before she fell asleep. The last thing she heard was Miss Polly singing a very mournful hymn through her nose; and, while she was wondering why it should keep people alive

A Dark Day. — Page 154.

to shake them, she passed into dreamland.
Very little good would such a heavy sleeper
have done if Miss Polly had had an ill turn.
It was Polly who was obliged to shake Dotty, and that rather roughly, before she could
rouse her.

"Where am I? Who is it?" said she.
"O, Miss Polly, are you dead?"

"Hush, child; don't speak so loud, or
you'll wake Abner. Little Katie is sick,
and I want you to stay with her while I
go down stairs and light a fire."

CHAPTER X.

THE END OF THE WORLD.

DOTTY shuddered. It seemed so unearthly and horrible to be awake at night; to see a lamp burning, and Katie looking so very white. It was the strawberries which had made her ill, as Miss Polly confessed. When that good but ignorant woman had gone down stairs, Dotty had much ado to keep from screaming outright.

"I thought somebody would die," said she to herself; "but I didn't s'pose it would be Katie. O, Katie, Katie Clifford! you're the cunningest child. We can't have you die!"

"Somebody leave me alone," moaned

Katie; "and 'twas you'n the Polly woman.
I don't love anybody in this world!"

"Darling! I didn't mean to," said Dotty,
"now honest. Polly said, 'O dear! she was
going to die'; but I might have known she
wouldn't. She told a wrong story — I mean
she made a mistake."

"You was naughty," said Katie, "velly
naughty; but you didn't meant to."

"No, Katie; 'twas Polly that was naughty."

"The krilt got off o' me," said Katie, picking at the tufted coverlet; "and then I was
sick."

"Miss Polly said it was the strawberries,
darling; and the cream poured over them
so thick."

"And getting into the watering-trough,"
added Dotty to herself, uneasily.

"Yes," sighed Katie; "'twas the stawbollies. Did *I* ask for the stawbollies? No,

but the Polly woman gave 'em to me. *I*
didn't want 'em; I wanted to be well."

After two weary hours, which seemed as
long as days almost, poor little Katie was
easier, and fell asleep. Dotty, who had tak-
en several naps in her chair, would now have
gone to bed again; but Miss Polly was
dressed, and said she could not close her
eyes if she tried; she meant to go down
stairs to her knitting. Dotty was afraid to
stay alone. She was always a little timid,
and to-night her nerves had been considera-
bly tried. The lamp cast frightful shadows,
and the newly-risen moon shone through the
white curtains with ghostly light. She
could "preach" to Jennie Vance about God's
"holding the whole world in his arms;" but
she could not always remember it herself.
She put on a white wrapper of Susy's, and,
looking like a wimpled nun, followed Polly

down stairs.   If she thought of wee Katie
at all, she thought there were good angels
in the room to guard her; but she could
not trust *herself* with them; she would rather keep close to Polly.

"I think," whispered Polly, unlocking the
back door and looking out at the sky, "it
must be very near morning; but the clocks
have both run down, and I can only guess at
the time by my feelings."

Then Polly made a brisk fire in the stove,
and set the tea-kettle to humming.

"Now I will get the milk-pail," said she,
"and you may put on the tea-pot.   I am faint
for want of something to drink."

It was one of Polly's peculiarities that she
always talked to children as if they had as
much judgment as grown people.   Dotty
did not know where to look for any tea-pot
except the very best one, which stood on a

shelf in the china closet; that she brought
and set on the stove, empty.

"Let me go too, let me go too!" cried
she, as Polly was walking out with the milk-
pails.

The daisies, with "their little lamps of
dew," seemed still asleep, and so did all the
"red-mouthed flowers" in the garden. The
cows looked up with languid surprise at
sight of their visitors, but offered no objec-
tions to being milked. Dotty gave one
hasty peep at the white hen sitting on the
venerable duck's eggs; but the hen seemed
offended. Dotty ran away, and took a sur-
vey of the "green gloom" of the trees, in
the midst of which was suspended the swing,
looking now as melancholy as a gallows.

"O, what a dreadful night this is!"
thought the child, standing bolt upright, lest
she should fall asleep. "Where's the sun?

He hasn't taken off his red silk night-cap.
He hasn't got back from China yet. Only
think, — if he shouldn't come back at all!
I heard somebody say, the other day, the
world was coming to an end. "Miss Polly,"
said she, aloud, reëntering the barn, "isn't
this the longest night you ever saw in all the
days of your life?"

"Yes, it has been considerable long, I am
free to confess," replied Polly, who thought
she had had a very hard time keeping house,
as was indeed the truth.

"Do you s'pose, Miss Polly, that some
morning the sun won't rise any more?"

"O, yes," replied Miss Polly, who was
always ready with a hymn : —

"'God reigns above, — he reigns alone;
    Systems burn out, and leave His throne.'

Why, yes, dear; the world will certainly
come to an end one of these days ; and *then*

11

the sun won't rise, of course; there won't be
any sun."

And Miss Polly began to hum one of her
sorrowful tunes, beating time with the two
streams of milk which dripped mournfully
into the pail.

"She is afraid this is the end of the world,"
thought Dotty, with a throbbing heart, and
a stifling sensation at the throat; "she don't
believe the sun is ever going to rise any
more."

The music suddenly ceased.

"These are very poor cows," said Polly,
in a reflective tone; "or else they don't give
down their milk. I understood you to say,
Dotty, that Ruth milked very early."

"If everything's coming to an end, it's no
wonder the cows act so," said Dotty to herself; but she dared not say it aloud.

They went into the house, the trail of

Susy's long wrapper following after little Dotty Dimple like the closing feet in one of Polly's long-metre verses. Still the moon shone with the same white, ghostly light, and the sun continued to keep away.

"This beats all," said Polly, mournfully, as she washed her hands, strained the milk, and set the pans away. "If I judged by my feelings, I should say it must be six o'clock, or very near it. At any rate, I'm going to have a cup of tea. What's this smell?"

On the stove stood a pool of something which looked like liquid silver, and proved to be the remains of the best tea-pot. At any other time Dotty would have felt very sorry; but now the accident seemed a mere trifle, when compared with the staying away of the sun. Who could tell "if ever morn should rise?"

Even Miss Polly, with her constitutional gloom, was not just now so miserable as Dotty, and never dreamed that it was anything but sleepiness which made the little girl so sober. Dotty was not a child who could tell all the thoughts which troubled her youthful brain.

"Well, well," said Polly, giving another inquiring glance at the sky; "not a streak of daylight yet! I'll tell you what it is, Dotty; we might as well go to bed."

But hark! As she spoke there was a loud report as of a pistol. It seemed to come from the cellar.

Miss Polly clapped both hands to her ears. Dotty shrieked, and hid her face in her lap, and shrieked again.

"It has come! It has come!" cried she, — meaning the end of the world, — and stopped her ears.

"What, what, what!" whispered Polly, in sore affright, walking back and forth, and taking snuff as she went. It was certainly startling to hear a pistol go off so unexpectedly, at that solemn hour, under one's very roof. Polly naturally thought first of housebreakers. She had barred and double-barred every door and window; but now she remembered with dreadful remorse she had not fastened the outside cellar door. No doubt it had been left open, and burglars had got into the cellar. O, what a responsibility had been put upon her! and why hadn't somebody particularly warned her to attend to that door? Perhaps the burglars were stealing pork. But they would not have fired a pistol at the barrel — would they? O, no; they were trying to blow up the house!

Polly took three pinches of snuff, one after the other, as fast as she could, slipped off her shoes, went to the kitchen window, and peeped through the blinds. Not much to be seen but moonlight, and the deep shadows of the ragged trees.

Another pistol-shot; then another. The sound came from that part of the cellar called the soap-room, directly under Polly's feet.

She did not wait for further warning. Every moment was precious. She meant to save what lives she could, for Polly was strictly conscientious. She took the nearly frantic Dotty into the china closet, dragging her like a sack of meal, and turned the key.

"Stay there, child, if you know when you're well off," whispered she through the keyhole. "The house is blowing up. I'm going to call Abner."

In her consternation Polly had not reflected that Dotty was as likely to be blown up in the closet as anywhere else. The unfortunate little girl screamed and struggled in her prison in vain. There was no way of escape. Night of horrors! As far as she was concerned, there were *two ends* to the world, and they were coming right together. Her agony is not to be described.

Abner came very soon; but it seemed an age. Being a brave man who had served three months in the army, he had the courage to walk down cellar and face the enemy.

He found nothing worse, however, than a few bottles of beer which had blown off their own heads. He brought them up in his arms.

"Here," said he, "are your burglars, with their throats cut from ear to ear."

"Well, if I ever had such a fright in all the days of my life!" cried Polly, staring at the bottles, and catching her breath.

Abner poured some of the beer into a goblet, and drank to the health of Miss Dimple, who climbed upon his knee, and felt as if the world had suddenly stopped coming to an end; and she was greatly relieved.

"But who fired the guns?" said she, not understanding yet what it all meant.

"It was only the beer coming out to get the air," said Abner, taking another glass. "You couldn't expect beer with the spirit of a hop in it to stay bottled up with a stopper in!"

"I never had such queer feelings," exclaimed Polly, rolling up her eyes; "and now it's all over, I feel as if I was going to faint away."

"I wouldn't advise you to," said Abner, coolly. "The enemy is routed, and victory is ours. Drink a little beer, Polly; it will revive your spirits. But what is the object, may I ask, of your prowling about the

house with this poor little girl at this hour
of night?"

"Why, what time is it? I thought by
my feelings it must have been daybreak long
enough ago."

It was Abner's private opinion that Polly would do well to think less of her "feelings" now and always; but he only said,
consulting his watch, —

"It's just one o'clock, ladies; time for
respectable people to be in bed."

Polly said she had never felt such surprise before in her life. She was afraid she
should be sick; for sitting up in the night
was always too much for her.

Dotty said her prayers over again, and
fell into a sleep "sweeter than a nest of
nightingales." And with her last waking
thought she thanked God the round red sun
was not worn out yet, **and the world had
not come to an end.**

CHAPTER XI.

CRAZY DUCKLINGS.

WHEN the family came home, Miss Polly had a most doleful story to tell about Katie's experiment in the watering-trough, the child's illness, the explosion of the beer, and her own fright and "dreadful feelings."

Mrs. Parlin regretted the loss of the tea-pot; Miss Louise said she had heard of "witches making tea," and perhaps this was the way they did it.

In return for Miss Whiting's laborious services in taking care of the children, Mrs. Parlin gave her various articles of food to carry home; for Polly had one room in Mr.

Grant's house, which she was accustomed to call her home, though she did not stay there very much. Polly sighed her gratitude, put on her dark bonnet, and said, as she went away, —

"Now, Mrs. Parlin, if it should so happen that you should all go away again, don't fail to ask me to come and keep house. You have always been so kind to me that I feel it a privilege to do any such little thing for you."

But in her heart poor Polly thought it was anything but a "little thing," and it cost her a great effort to promise to undertake it again. Mrs. Parlin thanked Miss Polly very politely; but for her part she thought privately it would be a long while before they would, any of them, be willing to trust such a nervous person with the care of the children a second time.

"Good by, all," said Polly, going off with
her double-covered basket on her arm; "remember me to Margaret when you write."

"What a funny thing to say!" remarked
Prudy; "how can we remember people to
anybody, or forget them to anybody either?"

"O, it was awful," said Dotty, linking arms
with Prudy and walking her off to the seat
in the trees. "Miss Polly scared me so I
don't believe I shall ever be afraid of lightning again!"

Little Flyaway ran after them, holding
her nipperkin of milk close to her bosom,
to keep off the flies, as she thought.

"I was defful sick," said she; "and did I
ask the Polly woman for the stawbollies?
No, she was naughty; *I* didn't wan't 'em.
She gived me stawbollies and stawbollies."

Prudy had to hear over and over again the
trials which both the children had suffered.

She had had a delightful time herself, as she
always did have, wherever she was. She
told Dotty and Flyaway of several interest-
ing events which had happened; but, best of
all, she had brought them a quantity of beautiful shells, which they were to divide with
Ruthie. The brisk Ruth had come back
again as energetic as ever. It proved that
her mother had not been so very ill,
after all.

"Bless that Prudy's little white heart,"
said she, kissing her on both cheeks; "she
never forgets anybody but herself."

Ruthie did not praise children as a general
thing; but she loved Prudy in spite of herself.

Aunt Maria had brought Dotty a beautiful
doll. "Because," said she, "I knew you
would try to take good care of my little
Katie."

"O, thank you ever so much, aunt 'Ria," cried Dotty, handing the dolly at once to Prudy to be admired. But next minute her conscience pricked her. She had no right to a present. True, Katie ought to have known better than to try to swim; still, as Dotty acknowledged, —

"I needn't have felt so sober, I s'pose, and then I should have taken care of her."

Dotty was learning to pay heed to these little pricks of conscience. Slowly and sadly she walked back to her aunt Maria, who was standing on the piazza training the clematis.

"I s'pose, auntie, you thought I took care of the baby; but I didn't. I let her swim. Miss Polly said *she* had the 'blues,' and so did I."

Aunt Maria smiled. "Very well," said she; "then keep the doll as a recompense for the suffering you have endured. I hope

you will not see two such gloomy days again
during the summer."

"O, you darling auntie! May I keep the
dolly?"

There was no sting now to mar Dotty's
pleasure in her new possession. Her
troubles seemed to be over; life was blos-
soming into beauty once more.

"Good news! Good news!" she cried,
rushing into the house, her head, with its
multitude of curl-papers, looking like a
huge corn-ball. "Two duckies have pecked
out!"

"You don't say so!" said Susy, coolly.
"High time, I should think!"

So thought the patient and astonished old
hen, who had been wondering every day for
a week if this wasn't an uncommonly "backward season." But at last the eggs, like
riches, had taken to themselves wings.

The soft, speckled creatures found plenty of admiring friends to welcome them as they tried their first "peep" at the world. They did not see much of the world, however, for some time, it must be confessed, on account of the corn-meal dough which the children sprinkled into their eyes.

"We won't let you starve, our ony dony Ducky Daddleses," said Dotty.

"Our deenty doiny Diddleses," said Katie after her, running hither and thither like a squirrel.

It was a time of great satisfaction. Dotty regretted that Jennie Vance had gone to Boston, for it would have been pleasant to see Jennie envious. What were gold rings compared to ducklings? The blunt little beaks pecked out very fast. As soon as they were all out, except the two eggs which were addled, the step-mother hen gathered

her family together and went to house-keep-
ing, gypsy fashion, in the back yard. She
clucked to the ducklings, and they followed
her, their little feet going pat, pat, on the
soft grass. A nice time they had, no doubt,
eating picked-up dinners, with now and then
a banquet of corn-meal dough. There were
eleven ducklings, five for Dotty, five for
Prudy, and one for Katie, the little girl with
flying hair.

After they had been alive two days, Prudy
thought they ought to have a bath; so she
took the large iron pan which Ruth used for
baking johnny-cakes, filled it with water, put
the tiny creatures in, and bade them "swim,"
to Madam Biddy's great alarm. They did it
well, though they were as badly crowded
as the five and twenty blackbirds baked in
a pie.

Katie wished the Charlie boy to see the

ducklings, which were "velly diffunt from
a piggie;" but. dear Charlie was very ill,
and when the children went with the milk,
they were not allowed to see him.

I may as well give you here the history of
the ducklings.

The next morning after their "swim" there
were only ten left, and Dotty's lamentations
could be heard all over the house. It was
Katie's odd one, she said, that was gone, the
one with a black picture on his back that
looked like a clover. Next morning there
were nine; and on the tenth day there was
but one solitary duckling left to pipe out his
sorrows all alone. The anguish of the children was painful to behold. Dotty's grief
affected her somewhat like the jumping
toothache. Who could have carried away
those dear, dear little duckies?

Who indeed? About this time the unprincipled old cat was found in the cellar, wiping her lips and purring over a little soft, speckled down.

"It was you that did it, was it, you wicked mizzable kitty?" burst forth the bereaved Dotty behind the swinging broomstick. "I must strike you with the soft end. I will! I will! If I'd known before that you'd eat live duckies! O, pussy, pussy, when I've given you my own little bones on a plate with gravy!"

"Whose little bones did you say, my dear?" asked Abner.

"Chickens and turkeys, and so forth!" replied Dotty, dancing about in her rage.

"Why, dear little damsel, do I really understand you to say you eat chickens? Then you are as bad as the cat."

"Why, Abner!"

"And worse, for you have no claws."

"No claws?"

"No — have you? If you had, I should conclude they had been made to tear little birds and mice in pieces."

"Is that what kitty's claws were made for?"

"So I am told. The truth is, she behaves much better for a cat than you do for a little girl."

Dotty scowled at her feet and patted them with the broom.

"And better than I do for a young man."

"But she ate my duckies — so there!"

"And Prudy's too," said Abner. "But Prudy doesn't beat her for it. It isn't pleasant to see nice little girls show so much temper, Dotty. Now I'm going to tell you something; all those ducklings were a little crazy, and it didn't make much difference what became of them."

"Crazy?"

"Yes, their minds were not properly balanced. There's one left, I believe. I'm going to make a lunatic asylum for him, and put him in this very day.

Dotty calmed herself and watched Abner as he made a pen with high stakes, and set in one corner of it a pan of water for swimming purposes.

The "speckling," as she called him, was Dotty's own; and when he was put into this insane hospital, all safe from the cat, his little mistress was in a measure consoled.

"I am sorry he is crazy," said she; "but I s'pose the hen didn't hatch him well. Maybe he'll get his senses by and by."

All this while dear little Charlie Gray was very ill. But I will tell you more about him in another chapter.

CHAPTER XII.

"THE CHARLIE BOY."

DOTTY heard of Charlie's illness every day; but, like all young children, she thought very little about it. Some one said he was "as white as his pillow." Dotty was amazed, for she had never seen any one as white as that. Then she heard her grandmother say she was "afraid Charlie would die."

"Die?" It sounded to Dotty like a word heard in a dream. She only knew that people must die before they went to heaven, and when they died they were very, very cold.

One night, when she went with the milk,

Mrs. Gray was weeping. She asked Dotty
if she would like to see little Charlie "once
more."

Dotty entered the darkened room with a
strange feeling of awe. There he lay, so
still she hardly dared to breathe. Darling,
darling Charlie!

But when she had touched the little hot
hand and kissed the sweet wasted face, her
heart grew lighter. What had made them
think he was going to heaven? He did not
look any more like an angel now than he
had always looked. His face was not as
white as the pillow; no, indeed; and he
was not cold; his lips were warmer than
hers.

"He used to have three chins once," whispered Dotty, "darling Charlie!"

"You love my little Charlie—don't you,
darling?" said Mrs. Gray; and then she

clasped Dotty in her arms and sobbed over
her; but Charlie did not seem to notice it.

"Yes, 'm, I do love him," said Dotty;
"Prudy says he's the cunningest boy there
is in this town."

And then she softly kissed Mrs. Gray's
cheek, though she had never kissed her before, and did not know why she was doing
it now.

"When he gets well, won't you let him
come to our house and play croquet? We
play it now with marbles, a teenty-tonty
game, and the wickets are made of hair-
pins spread out wide."

Dotty spoke very low, and Charlie did
not pay the least attention; but Mrs. Gray
sobbed still more, and held Dotty closer in
her arms, saying, —

"*Don't* talk so, dear!"

"How sorry you do feel to have him so

sick! He won't grow up, I s'pose, if he can't play. When he stays in bed it makes him grow littler and littler! Why, how little his neck is! It looks like a dandelion stem!"

"Don't, *don't*, dear child! Every word you say strikes right to my heart!"

Dotty looked up in Mrs. Gray's face with surprise. What had she said that was wrong? Perhaps she ought not to have talked about dandelions; she would not do it again.

"Dotty," said Mrs. Gray, looking sorrowfully towards the bed, "when fathers and mothers are not very wise, and do not know very well how to take proper care of their families, sometimes the Saviour calls their little children away."

Dotty knew what she meant now. She meant that Charlie was really going to heaven.

"O, Mrs. Gray," said she, "how Prudy and I will feel!" She would have said more, but was afraid she should make another mistake.

She kissed the unconscious little sufferer good by, though still it all seemed like a dream. Was this the same boy who had tried to wash the piggy? the same who had had meal-bags tied to his feet?

"A long kiss is a heart-kiss," she repeated to herself; and somehow she wondered if Charlie couldn't take it to heaven with him. Then she walked home all alone with her thoughts.

Next day they told her Charlie was dead. Dotty sat on the sofa for a long time without saying a word; then she went into the nursery, and staid by herself for an hour or two. When she returned she had her new doll in her arms, dressed in black. She wore a strip

of black crape about her own neck, and
had caught Flyaway long enough to put one
upon her arm, as well as upon the knobs
of the nursery doors.

"Prudy," said she, "it is polite to do so
when we lose people we love. Charlie was
my friend and Katie's friend, and we shall
treat him with the *respect* of a friend."

"Yes," said Katie, skipping after a fly,
"spec of a fend."

Dotty had never looked on death.

"You musn't be frightened, little sister,"
said Prudy, as they walked hand in hand to
Mrs. Gray's, behind the rest of their own
family, on the day of the funeral. "Charlie
is just as cold as marble, lying in a casket;
but *he* doesn't know it. The part of him
that *knows* is in a beautiful world where we
can't see him."

"Why can't we see him?" said Dotty,
peering anxiously into the sky.

"I don't know exactly why," replied Prudy, "but grandma Read says God doesn't
wish it. And He has put a seal over our
eyes, so an angel could stand right before
us, and we shouldn't know it."

"Ah!" said Dotty in a low voice; and
though she could see nothing, it seemed to
her the air was full of angels.

"But I think likely Charlie can see us,
Dotty, for the seal has been taken off his
eyes. O, it is beautiful to be dead!"

After this Dotty was not at all afraid
when she touched the cold face in the
casket, for she knew Charlie was not
there.

"It is beautiful to be dead!" said she next
day to Katie. "Charlie is very glad of it."

"Yes, he's in the ground-up, — in heav-
en!" said Katie in a dreamy way; for, in
her small mind, she believed heaven was a

place called "in the ground-up," and that
was all she cared about it.

"Yes, Charlie is in the ground," replied
Dotty, "but he doesn't know it. That dog
Pincher was put in the ground; but I think
likely *he* knew it, for his soul wasn't in
heaven; and he hadn't any soul; not a real
one."

"Well," said Katie, dancing out at the
door, "when will the Charlie boy come
back? I want um play."

"Why, Katie," said Dotty, in a tone of
reproof, "haven't I told you he is all
dead?"

"Well, YOU isn't dead — IS you? Less
us go an' swing!"

The little girls ran out to the trees, and
soon forgot all about their old playmate.
But, after this, whenever any one spoke of
Charlie, Katie thought, —

"The Charlie boy's in the ground-up, —
in heaven," and Dotty thought, —

"O, it is beautiful to be dead!"

———

For the present, we will leave them
swinging under the trees at grandma Parlin's; but if we see Miss Dimple again,
she will have been spirited away to her
own mother's home in the city of Port-
land.

CPSIA information can be obtained at www.ICGtesting.com
Printed in the USA
LVOW06s0227291015

460231LV00001B/89/P